PERFORM WITH
PURPOSE

A workbook for Athletic Mental Skills Training

RYAN DEFIBAUGH

ISBN: 9798374916553

DISCLAIMER

The contents of this workbook (worksheets, examples, text and graphics) are meant for general information only. The content is not intended to be a substitute for professional advice, diagnosis, or treatment. Always seek the advice of your mental health professional or other qualified health provider with any questions you may have regarding your condition.

If you are experiencing mental or emotional health concerns, please consult with your primary care physician or insurance provider for mental health counselors in your local area.

If you are in crisis or you think you may have an emergency, call your doctor or 911 immediately.

If you're having suicidal thoughts, call 9-8-8 to talk to a skilled, trained counselor at a crisis center in your area at any time (National Suicide Prevention Lifeline).

PHOTO CREDITS

All pictures used in this workbook were used with permission from the sites Unsplash.com, Canva Pro, or Techsmith.com/Camtasia. Below are specifics on each picture used in the Perform with Purpose Workbook:

DEDICATION

There are so many people I could recognize in this dedication, as I have learned from and been influenced by each and every person I have had contact with, directly and indirectly. So, please know, if our paths have crossed, if I have read one of your books, or listened to one of your podcasts, you have helped me grow into the person I am today.

Specifically, I would like to thank my wife Elizabeth for her love and support, my sons, Aidan, Landon, and Jacob for their curiosity, laughter, and helping me see the world in a truly optimistic manner. My parents, Craig and Diane for their incredible levels of patience, support and willingness to always lend a hand, and to my brothers, Chris and Sean, who are giving, loyal, and continue to push me to be my best.

Andrew Simpson and Dan D'Agostino, who both, in their own ways, encouraged me to move forward with my initial idea for this workbook.

Finally, the MBS Performance Counseling team, McKenna and Holly, my mentor counselor, Dr. Deb Phebus, and the most influential professor in my learning, Dr. Julia Orza.

Thank you!

HELLO FROM THE AUTHOR

Welcome to the Perform with Purpose Workbook! I am so excited to be a part of your personal journey as you navigate through the lessons, worksheets, and reflections in the following pages. By the end of the workbook, you will have learned how to create your Performance Mindset and approach the stressors that impact you in a purposeful manner.

I am Ryan Defibaugh, Owner of MBS Performance Counseling and a Licensed Clinical Professional Counselor (LCPC) as well as a Nationally Certified Counselor (NCC). Through my work with professional, college, high school, and middle school athletes, I have developed the Perform with Purpose approach. This methodology has been proven to help athletes of all ages and in all sports develop a powerful mental and emotional foundation for sport, school, and life.

The MBS Performance approach is unique in that it is built specifically for athletes. As a former college soccer player and former college coach at the Division I and Division III levels, I understand the demands of high-performance athletics and how important it is to train your mental and emotional skills, along with your physical ability.

This workbook was developed with you in mind and is meant to arm you with concepts, definitions, and action items you can begin using immediately to prepare for games and to manage performance anxiety, fear, doubt, worry, and pressure.

You are also invited to join our Perform with Purpose community, an online page where you can post questions, interact with other athletes, and get bonus materials such as monthly Zoom webinars, tips from our MBS Performance team-members, and more! You can join today by visiting our website at the link below and clicking on the "Join MBS Community" button:

https://mbsperformancecounseling.com/perform-with-purpose-workbook/

I look forward to being your guide as you navigate the lessons in this workbook. You have access to our team in the Perform with Purpose Community so please, ask questions, share your successes, and learn from others who have committed to their mental performance skills!

If you want to dive deeper into any of these topics or other areas of mental performance, you can visit our website at **https://mbsperformancecounseling.com/contact-us/** to setup an individual session with one of our counselors or mental performance coaches.

Congratulations on taking the first steps to **Perform with Purpose!**

TABLE OF CONTENTS

Daily Performance Plan: Pillar 4

INTRODUCTION

Welcome to the MBS Performance Counseling workbook! Throughout the following pages you will be asked to explore, define and make sense of your inner world so you are equipped to manage the external stressors that occur on a daily basis. The MBS Performance approach transforms how you see challenges, how you respond to mistakes, and how you prepare yourself for the athletic, academic, and life challenges you will face. By facing these challenges you will prove to yourself that you can do hard things. You will prove that you can overcome setbacks, you will prove to yourself that you can Perform with Purpose!

Athletes are not immune to the human condition!

Sports are played by people so it is fair, and obvious to state, that you deal with the same questions, issues, and doubt that anyone of us feel. You are not immune to anxiety, stress, depression, or feelings of inadequacy. In fact, it could be argued these are even more present in athletes. We are excited to see more professional, Olympic and college athletes speaking up about their own mental health journey. Training your mind and your emotions, along with the physical preparation in sport, allows you to not only play with more joy, but also to grow from challenges and play with more purposeful focus! You spend countless hours on the physical training involved in your sport. You spend years developing the technical skills required to perform at a high level and you practice game situations to grow your tactical understanding. However, the mental and emotional training necessary to compete at the highest level is largely ignored.

We want to create a new normal in the area of athletic mental health where it is part of the training for all athletes, coaches, clubs, high schools, and colleges. We see a future where it is not only okay to discuss these areas, but one where mental strength is developed purposefully. In this workbook, you will learn to transform your mental approach to challenges, to create a purposeful performance mindset, and how to enter your zone of optimal performance. By utilizing our workbook, you are taking the first step in discovering your passions, motivations, and purpose. Congratulations on committing to this journey and to achieving your personal greatness!

Imagine a soda bottle, unopened, sitting on the table. The contents inside of the bottle are settled, and if you opened the bottle at this point, there would be a bit of pressure released and the soda would be ready to drink. Now, can you imagine you are this bottle and the soda is a representation of your emotions? Think what happens when you are not settled and calm. Each time something stressful occurs during the day, your bottle gets shaken:

- You wake up late and have to rush to get to class on time...shake the bottle
- You did not get your homework done from the night before...shake the bottle
- Your teacher gives a surprise quiz...shake the bottle
- You have an argument with a friend...shake the bottle
- You read something negative on social media...shake the bottle
- You get a test back in math class, and did poorly on it...shake the bottle
- You get to practice and your mind is still stuck on the school day...shake the bottle
- You make a mistake in practice...shake the bottle
- Your coach yells at you...shake the bottle
- And this can go on throughout the day...shake the bottle

So, what does this mean? Why do I use this example to start the workbook? Well, would you open that bottle of soda after it had been shaken 10, 15, 20 times? What would happen? That is right, it would explode. Soda would bubble over and get on your hands, the table, the floor. It gets messy. Your emotions are the same way. If you let them build and do not have a purposeful approach to managing them, then you can explode. We see this in outbursts, shutting down during performances, walking away from the sport, and more. And, it can get messy!

How do you deal with the pressure that builds up through the day?

Think of that soda bottle once more. If you want to open it, knowing it has been shaken, knowing it could explode, what do you do? Open it just a bit, let some air out, close the lid, and repeat, right? Or, give it some purposeful time and come back once it is settled. Both strategies work for the soda, and if you think about it, both work for your emotional state. In this workbook, we will give you strategies and exercises to take a deep look into your purpose, your priorities, and into your mental and emotional framework. You will learn that you can take a purposeful approach to your daily life, both on and off the field, so you can thrive in response to stress, and learn to be purposeful in dealing with setbacks and success!

The MBS Performance Counseling Pillars

Our approach to developing your performance mindset is broken into 4 parts. This workbook will break each of these areas down and provide you with exercises to grow in each pillar. The first section will focus on **Self Discovery** where you will take time to delve into your motivations, your strengths, and who you are, as an athlete and as a person. Next you will learn how to incorporate **Positive Psychology** components into your performance, including optimism, resilience, grit, and gratitude. It is also important to identify the **Barriers to your Performance**, and how to overcome them. Finally, we will help you develop your **Daily Performance Plan** by identifying thoughts, emotions, and routines that can help prepare you for the demands of high-performance in sport, school, and life!

You are Enough!

At the core of our approach is a belief that you are exactly who you need to be, and that the person you are is good enough! We do not mean this as a reason to be complacent or to avoid challenges, but more so as a reminder that you, as a human being, are who you should be. You do not need to change who you are for anyone else or to try to fit in. We embrace this concept because we find athletes strive for results, strive to win, and attach happiness to results because they feel this makes them a good enough person. So, when these results are not perfect, you feel like you are not good enough as a person. But, you are already good enough. No result makes you a better person and no result makes you a worse person.

When you build from the foundation that you are good enough at your core, you are allowing yourself to stretch further for your goals and you are more willing to face challenges. By doing this, you are detaching from the fear of failure because failure is part of your journey, not an end result!

BUILD YOUR FOUNDATION

Your foundation is so important when it comes to dealing with adversity, setbacks, and what we call the external noise. But, what is your personal foundation and how do you go about discovering your internal strength?

Your foundation is the innermost version of you. It is where your core values, your purpose, your priorities, and your worldview are housed in your psyche. All of these components influence how you think, how you feel, and how you behave.

Later in the workbook, we will explore the importance of creating this foundation in order to prepare for, and respond to, high intensity moments like games, exams, and other life moments. By identifying your "why", understanding your priorities and creating your Performance Persona, you are being purposeful in developing who you are on and off the field. These are key components to becoming a consistent and mentally tough performer who can respond to success and adversity in a productive manner.

In order to build a strong, personal foundation, it is important to dive deep within yourself to understand your motivations, to question your current approach, and to detach from the fears and anxieties that guide you. You will hear me say throughout this book, your thoughts and feelings happen to you. You do not control them and you do not choose them. So, you will learn strategies to manage your thoughts/emotions and choose how you want to respond to them.

The Perform with Purpose workbook is meant to serve as an introduction to mental performance and provide foundational tools for you to apply to your performance in sport and in life. You will learn to:

- Define mindset terms
- Explore through Self-Reflections
- Instill Optimism, Resilience, Grit & Gratitude
- Understand Mental/Emotional Management
- Apply specific mindsets and emotional skills
- Track daily and weekly and monthly progress/feedback

MBS Performance Counseling, LLC

When it comes to mindset, our core philosophy at MBS Performance Counseling focuses on a unique combination of positive psychology, cognitive-behavior techniques, and a solution-focused approach. To begin our work with clients we first define mindset terms in an athlete-specific manner, skipping the psychological jargon. Therefore, we provide you with a definition you can understand and utilize in your own way. Our goal is to give you easily digestable information to utilize in your sport.

So what is Positive Psychology, Cognitive-Behavior, and Solution-Focused in terms of athletic performance?

Positive Psychology in short is an approach that focuses on strengths of the individual and encourages them to go beyond being "okay" or "not bad" in order to enter a level of thriving! In sport, this means giving yourself permission to reach beyond your comfort zone, letting go of the fear of losing, in order to reach higher levels. Some of the basic building blocks of positive psychology that we focus on at MBS Performance Counseling are Optimism, Resilience, Grit and Gratitude (these terms will be defined on the next pages).

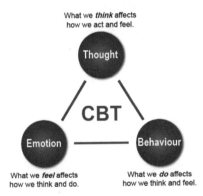

What we *think* affects how we act and feel.

Thought

CBT

Emotion — Behaviour

What we *feel* affects how we think and do.

What we *do* affects how we think and feel.

A Cognitive-Behavior approach focuses on the relationship between your thoughts, your emotions, and your behavior. When we explore your thinking and your feelings, you will find they drive your actions. For example, if you are afraid of losing, you will act more cautiously and take less chances. So, this workbook will help you understand your thoughts, recognize specific emotions, and decide which ones lead to a productive performance.

Solution-Focused means we will keep our attention on goals and creating solutions for you in the here and now. You will learn to look at your present thinking and actions and analyze them. From here, you will learn to ask yourself if your actions are productive or unproductive. If they are working for you, then we do not try to fix anything. If they are not working, we find solutions! It is all about you and creating your personal approach!

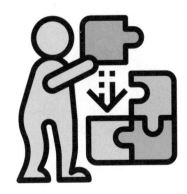

Self-Discovery: Pillar 1

"Knowing yourself is the beginning of all wisdom." – Aristotle

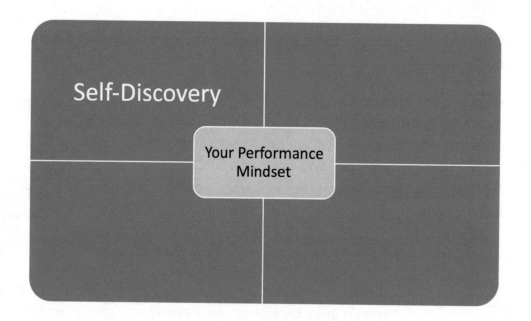

Self-Exploration

I firmly believe we are all capable of reaching our goals. One thing I have found through my work with people on and off the field, is that your internal approach is a major factor of whether you reach your goals.

With that said, it is so important to explore who you are!

This idea can be complicated though, right? Who you are is not a simple, one-word answer. More so, it is built through a series of experiences, influences, and expectations taught to you directly or indirectly throughout your life.

What is a direct influence? An example would be a coach talks to you about the expectations of hard work, being on time, and cleaning up the equipment after practice. You learn this value through a direct and purposeful lesson.

We are shaped by indirect lessons as well. An example of this is seeing a coach who does not complain about the referee, instead he or she focuses on how the team responds to a bad call, and on how the team can get set on defense in order to win the ball back. You indirectly learn to focus on what is in your control and to respect the calls of the referee by following the behavior modeled by your coach.

How we respond to challenges, setbacks, adversity, and success has been instilled in us piece by piece by the people around us. This includes our family, friends, classmates, teachers, neighbors, community, celebrities we see on television, we hear in music, and we follow on social media.

Our experiences shape the way we see the world around us.

In this topic, I challenge you to think about what you have learned from those around you. Are these positive, healthy, and helpful skills, thoughts, and views? Or, do they hinder you, create negativity and unhealthy thoughts and emotions?

The more you understand how you think, feel and act in relation to your experiences and surroundings, the more you can control how you define the world around you, and therefore how you respond to the success and failure you will encounter.

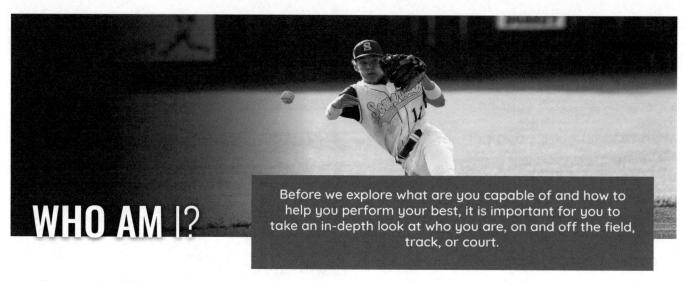

WHO AM I?

Before we explore what are you capable of and how to help you perform your best, it is important for you to take an in-depth look at who you are, on and off the field, track, or court.

What are the different roles you play in your life? *(son, daughter, friend, student, athlete)*

Do you adapt your behavior based on the role? How?

How optimistic/pessimistic are you?

1 is very pessimistic and 10 is very optimistic.

1	2	3	4	5	6	7	8	9	10

Are people inherently good or evil? Are they born this way or is it learned in life?

Do you think avoiding pain or chasing pleasure is a stronger motivator? Why?

When you feel stressed or anxious, how do you react? *(Thoughts, Emotions, Behaviors)*

MBS Performance Counseling, LLC

 **WHO** AM I?

How much of your time do you spend thinking about...

	1	2	3	4	5	6	7	8	9	10
The Future?										

	1	2	3	4	5	6	7	8	9	10
The Past?										

	1	2	3	4	5	6	7	8	9	10
The Present?										

Are you faithful? Is your God an active or passive God?
(An active God influences all events around you, a passive God created life, but leaves us to make decisions)

How do the following shape your views on success, confidence, and risk taking?
(Family, Social Class, Social Norms, Media, Religion)

How does who you are/your world view shape you as a person? As an athlete?

Roles and Values

The next area we want to identify are your values. In this exploration we are looking at your values as your standard of behavior that are important to you. Some of these might include trust, honesty, equality, etc.

On the next page, you will see the Roles and Values worksheet. Identify 5-10 values that you believe are important to you in your life. List these in the outer ring, surrounding your roles.

In step two, seek to understand where this value comes from. For example, if we chose honesty, maybe it came from your parents, maybe it was taught to you through your neighbors, or the societal norms you grew up with.

Finally, decide how you will purposefully practice this value on a daily basis so you live what you value.

The roles you play in your life are important to explore as well. We all play numerous roles in our lives, and identifying each one, allows us a deeper connection to who we are. If I ask who you are, how do you respond? Do you say you are an athlete? A brother? A sister? A student, a son, a daughter?

Why is it important to list all of the roles we play?

As we dive deep into training your mental and emotional approach to challenges, understanding that your overall well-being does not need to be attached to wins or losses in your sport, or perfect grades in school. Athlete, or student, are only two roles that make up your entire self-meaning. Even when one area of life has setbacks or challenges, we have others that are still thriving and strong.

Identifying with multiple roles provides you a strong support system off the field, which is important for growing resilience, grit, and a mentally tough approach to performance!

Roles and Values

1. In the outer ring, list the 6 values that matter most in your life (i.e. honesty, trust)
2. In the pie chart, use each section to list a role you play in life (i.e. son, friend, student)

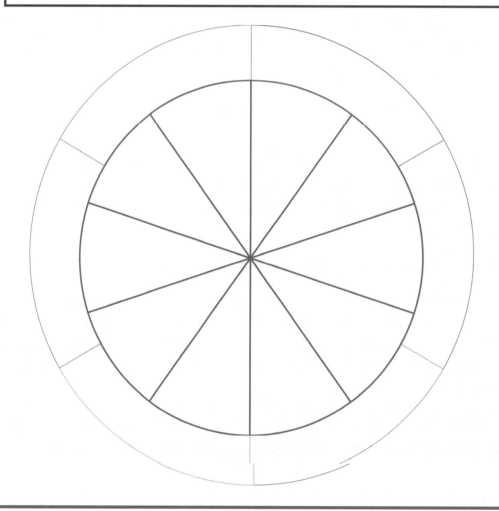

Reflections:

1. Are your values the same in sport as they are in your life outside of athletics?
2. What do your values reflect in you as person? Do you live by these values?
3. Where did you learn each value? Who or what in your life influences your value system?
4. When you look at all the roles you play in life, what thoughts do you have?

Living by Your Priorities

Defining your success is a combination of defining your 'Why', identifying your priorities and being purposeful with your time.

With this in mind, we want to go beyond your core values and begin to define your priorities in life.

Take a moment and brainstorm the areas that are most important to you in life. Is it family, friends, school, sport, spiritual growth, your health, etc.?

Who or what matter the most to you?

I want you to rank these in order of most important at #1, second most important at #2 and so on down the list for your top 7 priorities. Take a look at your list of seven. Do these all belong on the list? Are they in an order that represents your priorities? If so, I want you to cross out 4, 5, 6, and 7. Just one line through each will do, since they are obviously important to you having made the list in the first place.

Do the remaining top three make sense to you? If so, memorize these and take note of their order.

We focus on the top three because no one has time to fully manage 7 priorities.

When we try to manage too many priorities at once, we become overwhelmed, anxious, and negative. We begin to agonize that we cannot be everything to everyone.

At times, our priorities will conflict with each other. This forces us to make a choice between areas of our life that are important to us, and that choice can be difficult. By ranking our priorities, we are telling ourselves what is most important. We then have prepared ourselves for the decision before the conflict even occurs; reducing stress and allowing a clearer focus on our top priorities.

I recommend revisiting this exercise 2-3 times per year. The more you explore this and live each day by your priorities, the more you will define your path forward and understand the purpose behind your actions.

TOP PRIORITIES IN MY LIFE

In this exercise you will be asked to think about and record your top 7 priorities in life. What means the most to you when you think about all of the different roles you play in life?

RANKING	PRIORITIES

Review the list above, and rewrite your top three priorities. **Do your best to rank them in order of importance, with 1 being the most important.**

TOP 3 PRIORITIES
1 |
2 |
3 |

The second step in defining your success involves taking a time inventory. We do this with athletes by tracking their activity for 5 straight days in 30-minute increments. This inventory includes sleep, school, meals, sport, and anything else you spend your time doing.

Now, here is the eye-opening part.

Compare your time inventory to your priority list.

How much of your time each day is spent on your top 3 priorities? How much time is spent on your 4-7 priorities? How much time is spent on activities not even represented on your priority list?

I've done this activity with a large number of individuals and teams, and no one has ever put their cellphone, or scrolling through TikTok, on their priority list, however, often our time inventory shows 4-5 hours, or more, on a cellphone each day.

Imagine if we turned those hours into time focused on our top priorities.

If, for example, your family is a top priority, imagine spending 1 more hour per day on strengthening your family bonds. If school is a priority, imagine dedicating 1 more hour on your studies and 1 more hour on your sport.

One more hour per day can lead to huge growths in any area. It is powerful to be purposeful with your time and this activity is one of the best ways to fully understand what matters to you!

A discrepancy between your priorities and your time inventory basically means one of two things: You need to shift how you spend your time, or the priorities you identified are not really your priorities.

Finally, it is also important to take a person inventory.

The people we allow into our lives are strong influences over our mindset.

Who do you spend most of your time with?

- Who pushes you to be better, to reach beyond your comfort zone, to be the best version of yourself?

- Who seems to always bring positive energy to every situation?

- On the other hand, who holds you back, puts you down does not believe in your dreams? Who seems to always be focused on the negative and is always complaining?

This negative energy affects you.

Who you give your time, energy, and emotions to is important, so choose wisely!

A smaller group of really personal, positive relationships are so much more powerful than having a larger friend group of people who do not connect deeply. I call these "surface relationships" because you have no idea who they are, what motivates them, or what they fear.

A team who has not taken the time to get to know each below the surface, will not be as resilient as a team who has taken purposeful time to understand each of its members. Breaking down your priorities and inventories, you should now have an idea of your priorities, how you spend your time, if your time matches your priority list and the positive people in your life.

 **TAKING PERSONAL** INVENTORY

CONNECTING PRIORITIES TO TIME INVENTORY

How many hours per day do you spend on your top 3 priorities?

How many hours per day do you spend on your bottom 4 priorities?

How many hours do you spend on activities not on your list?

PEOPLE INVENTORY

Who is a positive influence in your life?

Who pushes you to achieve your goals?

Who can brighten your day no matter what is going wrong?

Who holds you back from being your best?

Who is a negative influence on you?

Who makes you feel negative emotions or think negative thoughts more often than positive?

Who talks you out of your goals or doubts you?

TAKING PERSONAL INVENTORY

REFLECTIONS

Does your time spent per day reflect your priorities?

If not, does your time need to change, or are your listed priorities inaccurate?

Do you spend more time with people who inspire you, or with people who hold you back?

MBS Performance Counseling, LLC

Define Your Why

"He who has a why to live for can bear almost any how." – Friedrich Nietzsche.

I love working with athletes on this component of the MBS Performance Approach. Exploring Your Why is something we often forget to do as athletes. We know we enjoy our sport so we find a team, show up to practice, and compete in the games. But why? As our competition gets stronger, the demands get greater, and the sacrifices become larger, why do we continue to push ourselves to be our best? Why do we give up time with our loved ones to pursue our sport? Why do we sacrifice time doing other activities we love, in order to give more to our sport? Do we make these sacrifices? I believe the process of building our "why" allows us to build a strong foundation. It is a centering concept that we can refer to when we are challenged and pushed to our max.

With a well-defined why, these challenges will be welcomed, instead of feared. However, we must first understand ourselves, our motivations, why we play, and why we compete, before we can expect to overcome setbacks and learn from adversity. Without defining our why, we will lack the motivation to push to our highest level of competition. So, how do we determine our "why"?

When we work with athletes, developing your why is broken into 4 components:

- **Passion (ignition)** - what made you first fall in love with your sport?
- **Expectations** - what do you expect to achieve in your sport?
- **Motivation** - what makes you show up everyday to train, even when your goals are not guaranteed?
- **Sacrifices** - what do you give up for your sport? Are you ok with these sacrifices?

THE FOUR COMPONENTS OF OUR WHY

BREAKING DOWN YOUR WHY

EXPECTATION | What do you hope to accomplish in your sport?

PASSION | What ignited your love of the game?

MOTIVATION | What drives you to work your hardest everyday?

SACRIFICE | What do you give up to focus on your sport?

Positive Psychology Mindset: Pillar 2

*"If my mind can conceive it and my heart can believe it -
then I can achieve it." – Muhammad Ali*

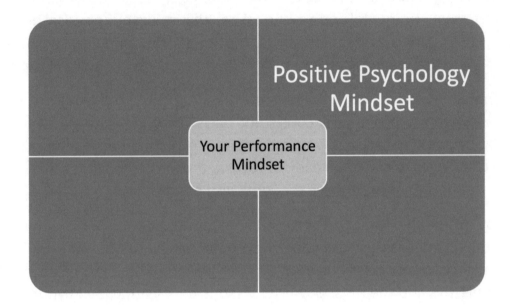

POSITIVE PSYCHOLOGY MINDSET

Building a positive mindset is key in dealing with barriers to your performance, which we will explore later in the workbook. In this section, we will break down the 4 components of positive psychology; Optimism, Resilience, Grit, and Gratitude.

Together, these concepts allow you to develop hope, respond to setbacks, pursue your goals over time, and be thankful for the success and failure you encounter along the way.

Positive Psychology challenges the idea that we should only seek help when something goes wrong. We often treat our mental and emotional health just like our physical health. We strive to feel "okay", "fine", and my all-time favorite, "not bad." We define our well-being through the absence of negative feeling and only seek help when we fall below the "okay" threshold.

Positive Psychology says you can look beyond "okay" and build the mental and emotional skills that allow you to thrive on a consistent basis. Through purposeful self-talk, visualization, and being solution-focused, you can choose to build a purposeful plan to wake-up ready for the challenges of the day, ready to receive the successes that are available to you, and to better respond to unproductive thoughts and emotions.

We will start by exploring optimism since this is the foundation for positive mindsets. By creating a belief that change is possible, you will be more willing to bounce back from adversity (resilience) and stick to your passions over a longer period of time (grit). This section may be my favorite to discuss and the most powerful lessons for creating joy in your life!

MBS Performance Counseling, LLC

Optimism

This is a basic foundational block to our approach. Optimism is not just thinking positive and it is not just thinking everything is perfect. In fact, we focus on the following components of Optimism

1. Change is possible
2. Your actions matter to create change
3. Good outcomes are possible
4. Setbacks are temporary
5. Focus on what is in your control

Pessimism

This is the opposite of optimism. It is a feeling of being stuck, lack of hope, and feeling like you cannot affect change in your life. Pessimistic thinking can lead to higher levels of anxiety and depression.

1. Change is NOT possible
2. Your actions do not matter
3. Good outcomes are NOT possible
4. Setbacks are permanent
5. Everything is out of your control

Athletes often understand this concept in the physical sense, but is important to utilize optimism for our preparation and response to setbacks as well.

- Am I more likely to take a risk on the field if I believe it will work out?
- Will I recover from a mistake quicker if I know I can take actions to create change?
- If I know a mistake or a result is temporary can I get over it more effectively?
- What will change if I focus only on what I can control instead of what I cannot?
- You believe "If I practice this skill, I will be able to improve it."
- Is the mental and emotional approach to sport a skill you can develop?

Examples of Optimism in Sports

The track runner who focuses on her own strategy and technique instead of worrying about the time of her opponents.

The soccer player who had the ball taken from him in the last 1v1, but continues to dribble at the defender knowing he can get by him next time.

The basketball player who knows that one missed shot does not mean he will miss the next one. He continues to look for scoring opportunities.

OPTIMIST VERSUS PESSIMIST

EXAMPLE | It is so important to learn how to adopt an optimistic mindset so you can overcome challenges and remain solution-focused. Read the difference in Optimism and Pessimism in the first row of side by side squares.

OPTIMISTIC OUTLOOK	VS	PESSIMISTIC OUTLOOK
• Your team is going forward into the attack, you cut by a defender, receive a pass and shoot at the goalie, but miss the goal. The optimist in you refocuses, you remind yourself that setbacks are temporary, just because you missed this shot does not mean you will the next one. So you quickly access how to get the ball on goal next time. • You turn to your teammate and acknowledge the good pass they made to you. You get back on defense and contribute to winning the ball back and creating the next change!		• Your team is going forward into the attack, you cut by a defender, receive a pass and shoot at the goalie, but miss the goal The pessimistic thinker drops your head, you believe you will never score and you start to that your coach and teammates no longer believe in your ability. You feel like you should not even make the runs to goal anymore because you feel like you will not score anyway. • You find yourself looking to create an excuse, "the ball bounced weird, the field stinks, it was a bad pass." You forget to defend and your opponent goes down the field and scores.

EXERCISE | Next, think about a recent example from your own competition and explore the difference between an optimistic outlook and a pessimistic viewpoint. Which one will help you achieve your performance goals most often?

OPTIMISM PERSONAL EXAMPLE	VS	PESSIMISM PERSONAL EXAMPLE

Growth Mindset

You most likely have heard, or will hear, someone talk to you about a growth mindset versus a fixed mindset. Basically, these are terms that can be defined through optimism and pessimism. A growth mindset believes you can create change, that you are in a process of development, and your actions and mindset can create new opportunities. A fixed mindset believes the opposite. This way of thinking believes that change is not possible and 'you are who you are' or 'it is what it is.' There is no reason to put in the effort to create change, because no matter what you do, nothing will ever be different than how it is right now.

> **You are not born optimistic or pessimistic just as you are not born with a growth mindset or fixed mindset!**

VS

(For each category check whether you are more growth or fixed mindset)

Growth Mindset		Fixed Mindset
Willing to fight through obstacles ◯	**Obstacles**	◯ See obstacles as a reason to quit
Welcome challenges as a way to grow ◯	**Challenges**	◯ Fear challenges and look to avoid them
Believes that effort breeds mastery ◯	**Effort**	◯ Sees effort as useless and meaningless
Celebrates the success of others and is inspired by them ◯	**Success of Others**	◯ Gets jealous and feels threatened by success of others
Seeks out criticism and uses it to grow ◯	**Criticism**	◯ Avoids or ignores criticism and makes excuses

CREATING ALIGNMENT

What is alignment?

Your performances are made up of a combination of your mental, emotional and physical skills. The more these skills are able to operate together, the more consistent your performances will be. In terms of alignment, we want you to create a singular focus for your mental, emotional and physical energy.

Why does this matter in sports?

Imagine playing in a tough game. Your physical skills have been developed for this moment through the previous games and the practices your coach has created for you. However, some events happen during the game that disrupt your mental and emotional focus. First, the referee calls a foul against you that you think was a bad call. You feel frustrated and angry and your thoughts start to focus on how bad of a call it was. Soon after this call, you make a beautiful pass to a teammate who misses an easy scoring opportunity. Your frustration increases as does your anger. You yell at your teammate and throw your hands up in the air in disgust. Your head drops and you start thinking your team will never score and there is no chance you will win this game.

How are you, in this example, out of alignment? How can you refocus your mental and emotional energy? How does this connect to optimistic thinking?

_____

_____

_____

_____

_____

_____

_____

> This divide in your physical, mental, and emotional energy will hinder you from performing to the best of your ability. Throughout this workbook, you will learn strategies that help you align these three areas.

MBS Performance Counseling, LLC

What is in my **control?**

As mentioned on the previous page, being out of alignment can zap your energy. You spend so much time and energy (mental, emotional, and physical) trying to control every aspect of your life. However, as we discussed in optimistic thinking, it is important to understand what is in your control, and what is not in your control. You can align your physical, mental and emotional focus more consistently when you spend your time on the factors you can control or influence.

Use the chart below to track one week of your life. First identify areas in school, sports, relationships, etc that are in your control, and then do the same for what is out of your control. Then, rate each item on how well you take responsibility for the factors under your control.

I can control	Mon	Tues	Wed	Thurs	Fri
1. *ex. My attitude*	8	7	8	6	9
2.					
3.					
4.					
5.					
6.					
7.					

I cannot control

1. *ex. Calls by the referee*
2.
3.
4.
5.
6.
7.

What distracts you from focusing on what is in your control? How can you productively respond to this distraction?

_____

_____

_____

Resilience

You have probably heard the term resilience often as an athlete, but, have you ever defined it? Resilience, in short, is the ability to bounce back after a setback. How quickly can you get back on track towards your goal when something goes wrong?

I also believe we have to be resilient in our efforts when things are going well. How often do you see a team relax once they score only to have the other team come down the field and score within the next few minutes? Resilience in the end, is about mental and emotional maturity as well as creating a balanced response to the highs and lows we experience as athletes and in our lives off the field.

Adopting an optimistic mindset is the first step in building resilience. You have to truly believe setbacks are temporary. You must believe you can take action to continue towards your goal before you can apply resilience in your life.

I love resilience because it is earned through action. You cannot build resilience purely by reading a book, having a coach tell you to be resilient, and a parent can't do it for you. You cannot even develop resilience through this course alone. By understanding the concept, you are one step closer to taking a purposeful approach to errors, mistakes, and failures; deciding to be solution-focused and get back to a positive attitude quickly. This can only be done by working through setbacks as they arise, reframing disappointment and frustration into excitement and patience.

A resilient athlete is:

1. Solution-focused
2. Confident in his or her skills and ability
3. Process over result oriented
4. Embraces failure as a learning tool
5. Playing to Win versus not to lose

What is playing to win versus not to lose? There is a major difference in this mindset approach. When you approach the match with a play to win attitude you are confident, thinking about the possible good outcomes, rather than what can go wrong. You are much more willing to take healthy risks in order to achieve your goals. On the other hand, playing not to lose makes you adverse to risks. You are worried about making mistakes. You see competition as a threat and usually have higher levels of anxiety on match days. We develop a play to win mentality through our positive self-talk, defining our goals, adopting resilient responses to adversity, and positive imagery prior to the match.

How do we develop resiliency?

1. Don't blame, instead ask, "Now What?"
2. Use the power of "yet"
3. Develop an individual mantra
4. Avoid using "I am" statements in a negative manner
5. Surround yourself with a strong support system
6. Practice your productive responses to adversity

In summary, embrace the fact that you will make mistakes. Enjoy the learning that comes out of both success and failure!

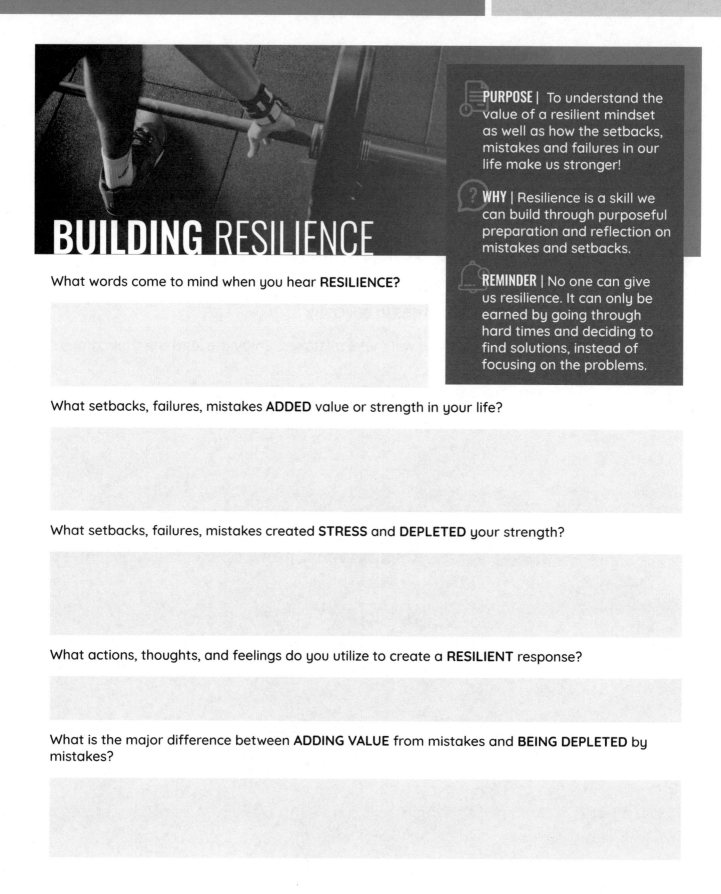

BUILDING RESILIENCE

PURPOSE | To understand the value of a resilient mindset as well as how the setbacks, mistakes and failures in our life make us stronger!

WHY | Resilience is a skill we can build through purposeful preparation and reflection on mistakes and setbacks.

REMINDER | No one can give us resilience. It can only be earned by going through hard times and deciding to find solutions, instead of focusing on the problems.

What words come to mind when you hear **RESILIENCE?**

What setbacks, failures, mistakes **ADDED** value or strength in your life?

What setbacks, failures, mistakes created **STRESS** and **DEPLETED** your strength?

What actions, thoughts, and feelings do you utilize to create a **RESILIENT** response?

What is the major difference between **ADDING VALUE** from mistakes and **BEING DEPLETED** by mistakes?

Grit

Grit is similar to resilience in that it is a mentality that keeps you focused on your goals. However, where resilience is how quickly you bounce back from adversity, grit is the ability to stay focused on the same or similar goal over an extended period of time. A lot of people put hard effort in over a short time and think that will lead to their desired outcome, however, when you study high achievers in athletics and other fields, these are people who have the emotional maturity to push themselves day in and day out over years, sometimes decades, to achieve their goals.

In her book, Grit, Angela Duckworth explains grit in a two-part equation:

Talent x Effort = Skill

Skill x Effort = Achievement

Notice how effort counts twice towards achievement? Grit depends on the consistent effort over time for talent to become skill and skill to lead to achievement.

Combining the three positive psychology concepts we have explored, we can see the flow from optimism to resilience to grit. When you embrace optimism and believe setbacks are temporary, you are more likely to employ resilience when faced with adversity. Grit is optimism and resilience at work over a longer period of time on a consistent basis. So what makes you a gritty athlete? What are your major goals as an athlete? Are you willing to bring positive energy to your training each day in order to achieve them? Are you willing to fail, get back up and try again every day? When others doubt you, or you hit a roadblock, will you keep pushing forward? Are you putting in the purposeful practice with the necessary effort to hone your natural talent? Are you willing to make continuous sacrifices to concentrate your effort in order to achieve in your sport?

Now, take the concepts of resilience and grit and tie them back to your priorities list. If you have priorities more important than your sport, you may not be willing to sacrifice them to grow in your athletics pursuit, and this is okay! The important part is to be genuine to yourself and understand where you want to go in your journey, what you want to achieve, and how you are willing to get there.

What are your athletic goals?
Are you willing to pursue these
through the ups and downs over time?

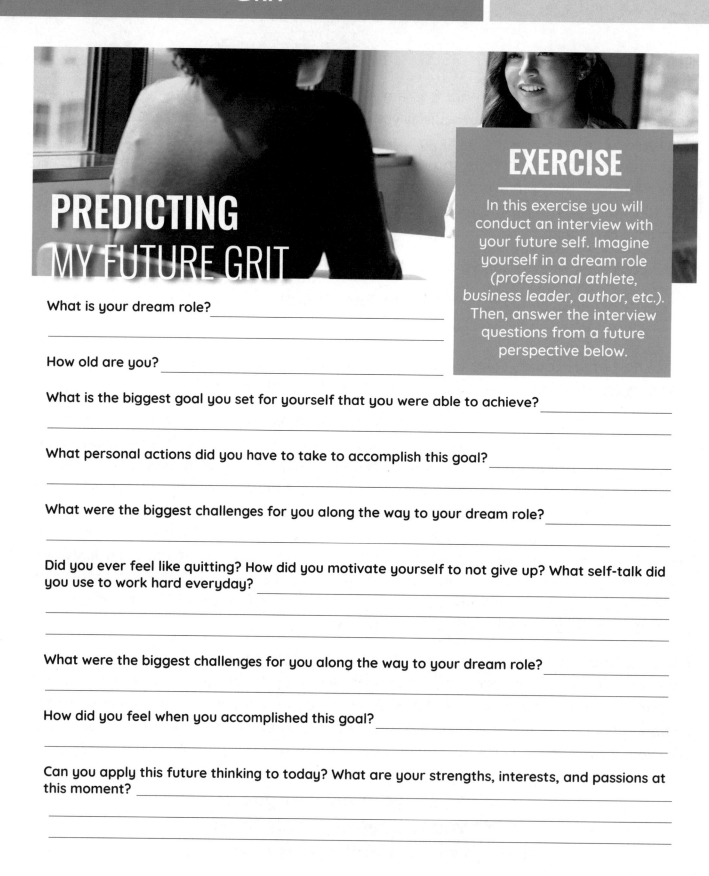

PREDICTING MY FUTURE GRIT

EXERCISE

In this exercise you will conduct an interview with your future self. Imagine yourself in a dream role (*professional athlete, business leader, author, etc.*). Then, answer the interview questions from a future perspective below.

What is your dream role? _____

_____

How old are you? _____

What is the biggest goal you set for yourself that you were able to achieve? _____

_____

What personal actions did you have to take to accomplish this goal? _____

_____

What were the biggest challenges for you along the way to your dream role? _____

_____

Did you ever feel like quitting? How did you motivate yourself to not give up? What self-talk did you use to work hard everyday? _____

_____

_____

What were the biggest challenges for you along the way to your dream role? _____

_____

How did you feel when you accomplished this goal? _____

_____

Can you apply this future thinking to today? What are your strengths, interests, and passions at this moment? _____

_____

_____

Gratitude

Gratitude is one of the most powerful traits one can adopt. The overall peace you feel when you fully appreciate your circumstance, opportunities, and the people around you cannot be matched by many other mindset components.

Have you ever stopped to think about all of the pieces that fit together to get you where you are today?

How many times do you stop to consider how fortunate you are to be walking on to the field each day, to have the opportunity to play your sport? To have a field or court to play on? To have the necessary equipment? To have your health and the friendship of teammates?

Often, we fail to think of all the areas we are grateful for because we do not take the time to think about it. Either we are too busy in our minds or we are just used to all of the necessities being there for us.

Imagine if we spent more time recognizing what we are grateful for, instead of spending time thinking about our worries, fears, and doubts.

I encourage you to take a moment each day and think about all of the things and people you appreciate. How do you do this? Below are three simple ways:

1. Daily gratitude check – at night before bed, record 2-3 things, events, people you appreciate and/or what went well.

2. Gratitude Walk – Take a 30-minute walk where you think only of the appreciation you have for your life and the people you have in your inner circle.

3. Gratitude Letter – Write a letter to someone you appreciate. Specifically, thank them for the areas where they have impacted your life for the better! For the brave souls out there, share this letter with the person. For the bravest of souls, read it to them in person so you can see and feel their reaction and they can see and feel your appreciation. It is powerful!!

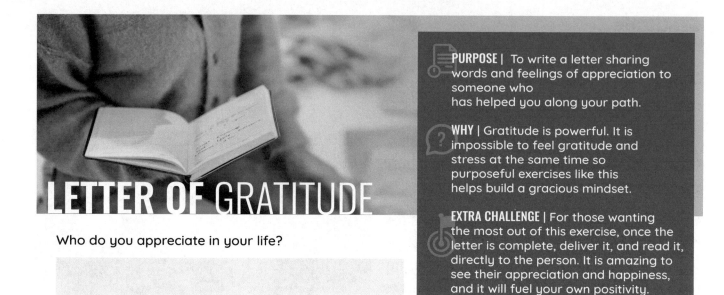

LETTER OF GRATITUDE

PURPOSE | To write a letter sharing words and feelings of appreciation to someone who has helped you along your path.

WHY | Gratitude is powerful. It is impossible to feel gratitude and stress at the same time so purposeful exercises like this helps build a gracious mindset.

EXTRA CHALLENGE | For those wanting the most out of this exercise, once the letter is complete, deliver it, and read it, directly to the person. It is amazing to see their appreciation and happiness, and it will fuel your own positivity.

Who do you appreciate in your life?

What are some of the main reasons?

AREAS TO CONSIDER WHEN WRITING YOUR LETTER

	Emotions you feel about this person	Specific areas of thanks for him or her	His or her impact on your life	How you will put their lessons to work
PERSON 1				
PERSON 2				
PERSON 3				
PERSON 4				

Barriers to Performance: Pillar 3

Obstacles don't have to stop you. If you run into a wall, don't turn around and give up. Figure out how to climb it, go through it, or work around it." – Michael Jordan

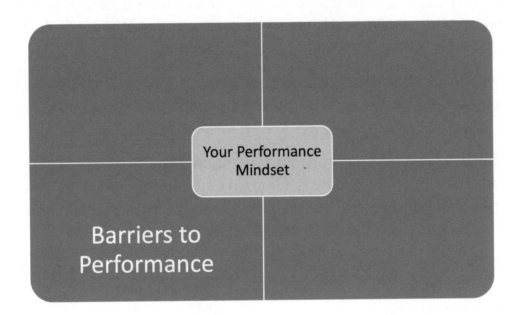

What is Anxiety

When we talk about anxiety, it is important to realize there is a difference between anxiety as a diagnosable disorder and anxiety as a natural emotion.

The Diagnostic and Statistical Manual of Mental Disorders (DSM-5) defines Anxiety as "excessive anxiety and worry (apprehensive expectation), occurring more days than not for at least 6 months, about a number of events or activities (such as work or school performance). The anxiety, worry, or physical symptoms cause clinically significant distress or impairment in social, occupational, or other important areas of functioning."

The above definition is the clinical definition of General Anxiety Disorder, which is a diagnosable level of anxiety, occurring over months to years, that impacts the daily life of the individual.

On the other hand, anxiety as a natural human emotion is characterized by feelings of worry, fear, and dread. As mentioned, anxiety is a human emotion that we all feel at varying levels. At MBS Performance Counseling we use the following as our working definition of anxiety for our clients, "anxiety is our response to a perceived threat."

We find this definition is digestible, clear, and concise. It allows you to understand the key concepts of how we work with anxiety. First, it is a response, and second, it is triggered by the feeling of possible danger.

In this way of thinking, you are allowed to see the purpose behind anxiety and anxious thinking. Anxiety can be seen as a positive response system in your body, even though it feels uncomfortable, since it serves as an alert to possible danger. If anxiety had a voice, it would be saying "uh-oh, you need to pay attention to this because it could be a danger to you." One important word here is "could." The perceived threat is not guaranteed to happen.

Taking this a step further, our brain's first job is survival. So, when we perceive a threat our brain's priority is to survive the danger. If anxiety is our response to this threat, then anxiety is actually an important system in identifying, preparing, and surviving threats.

Stop here for a second and think about the physical symptoms you feel while anxious.

1. _____

2. _____

3. _____

4. _____

5. _____

6. _____

7. _____

Most often, these physical symptoms can make you feel scared, worried, and more anxious. You start to worry that something is wrong with you, which usually then makes these symptoms even stronger. As this cycle continues, you may find yourself only thinking about what will go wrong and in turn, believing it will go wrong.

So, let's take a look at the list below and see if they match the symptoms you notice in yourself.

1. *increased heart rate*

2. *increased breathing rate*

3. *dry mouth*

4. *fidgeting/jittery*

5. *stuck on negative thought*

6. *feeling you have to get away*

Is this list similar to the symptoms you feel when anxious?

As discussed above, these symptoms can make you feel like something is wrong, and when unchecked, can cause panic in our mental response.

What if I was to tell you all of these symptoms that usually create more worry, are a sign of your body working exactly as it should? Each of these symptoms, or responses, plays a purposeful role in helping you deal with a threat. Even though they feel uncomfortable, your body is priming you to deal with the perceived danger.

When you label something as a threat, your brain prepares your body to act in order to survive. Remember, your brain's first priority is survival. So, anxiety is in fact your survival system being activated. Knowing these symptoms serve a purpose is important for being able to challenging our unproductive negative thoughts. Can you label anxiety as your "Alert System" instead of a negative feeling?

Since the brain focuses on survival first, it likes to understand the surrounding environment and it likes to be able to predict what is around the corner. This is why anxiety lives in the future. It is a worry about what might happen, or fear of the unknown.

Our brain is so incredible in many ways, but it absolutely stinks at predicting the future. You may notice your brain's default in thinking about future events, is that it goes to worst-case scenario, especially in stress inducing areas such as school, test performance, and sport performance. Your brain is simply trying to prepare you to deal with the possible danger of the worst-case. However, you believe what you are thinking, so you believe the worst-case is inevitable instead of just a possibility.

This cycle becomes detrimental to our mental and emotional health and in turn, our performance. So, how do we break this cycle and respond to the anxious thinking?

Step back for a minute now and think of a situation where your thoughts went straight to what will go wrong. Did you believe these thoughts? Did they make you fear the upcoming situation? Think of how many times you have feared an upcoming experience and once you were there, you realized it was not bad at all. In fact, you found you actually enjoyed the very thing you were afraid of before you experienced it.

Now, picture this conversation with one of your friends:

You: "I have a big game tomorrow that will determine if we make the playoffs"

Friend: "Uh-oh, you are not ready for this game. You are going to make mistakes and let your team down. They will probably be mad at you since it will be your fault your team did not make the playoffs."

How would you respond to this friend? Are you going to accept their version of the future?

Probably not! You will most likely be upset with them and tell them why their comments are not helpful.

But, when your brain tells you these same comments you accept them. You believe them as truth and panic over the impending doom.

Why can't you challenge your own brain, your own thoughts, just like you would challenge your friend in the above example?

Well, you can! But, before you are fully equipped to put the work into challenging your negative thinking, it is important to understand how your body is actually responding to the "perceived threat."

Below, we will briefly explore the biological responses in your brain and body:

When your brain recognizes a threat, it activates the release of cortisol, your stress hormone. The release of cortisol sparks certain responses in your body, all of which serve the purpose of surviving the perceived threat.

Your survival response in this case can be looked at through the Fight or Flight lens.

Do I run or do I fight in order to survive the threat?

In the case of a physical threat, this can be pretty simple to understand. Picture you are on a hike in the woods; the leaves are changing colors, the air is cool and crisp, you can hear the moving water of a river in the distance, and the views over the cliff to your right are spectacular. Your eyes catch something moving on the path and as you look up, you see a bear about 30 yards ahead of you.

Is this a perceived threat?

I would say so!

Your brain labels the bear as a threat so cortisol is released in your body, activating your Fight or Flight system. The brain is getting ready to survive this potential threat by preparing your body for action. Should you punch this bear in the face, or should you run? Either way, your body needs to activate or prime your muscles for high-capacity action.

A quick side note: your response to a threat is the same whether that threat is physical, emotional, social, academic, or athletic. In fact, your response is the same even when the threat is perceived and not real!

So, now we can look at this response in regards to the physical symptoms we identified earlier in this section:

Increased heart rate

When cortisol is released, our body responds by increasing the blood flow to our muscles, pumping more blood through the body, bringing oxygen to our muscles so they are prepared for action, whether that is to avoid or confront the threat.

Increased breathing rate

Similarly, the release of cortisol sparks the body to send oxygen to all your major muscles. Again, this is preparing you to act.

Jitteriness/Fidgeting/Feeling that you have to move

As mentioned in the previous two examples, cortisol release sends oxygen to all of your muscles, and they are now ready to act. But, when you are at your desk before a test or in the car before a game, where do you put that energy? Your body is saying "run!, fight!, move!" but you may not be able to release that energy in that moment so you are fidgeting with pent up, nervous energy.

Dry mouth

Saliva is the first step in the digestion process. When you are faced with a threat, your brain no longer cares about breaking down food, so the water/oxygen of saliva is repurposed to your muscles, again preparing for action to survive the threat.

Stuck on the negative thought

When you are faced with a threat, the brain is able to filter out everything else. In our bear in the woods example, our brain no longer cares about the beautiful views, the sound of the river, or the color of the leaves. It wants to focus on the perceived threat, so that you can survive it. So, you focus on that bear. Does it see you, does it look angry, is it coming closer, is it walking away, are cubs nearby? Since our anxiety response is the same for other types of threats as well as physical threats this same concept is true when we focus on the negative thoughts surrounding a social situation, a test at school, or an athletic performance.

Now that you have a deeper understanding of anxiety, why you feel it, and how your body reacts, we will look at how this applies in your athletic performance and how we can manage these thoughts and feelings effectively. Remember, at its core, anxiety is a natural human response to help you identify potential threats and survive them. The physical symptoms you experience in response to anxious thinking have a purpose as well. It is important to remind yourself that you are okay. Instead of fearing the symptoms you feel, the next step is identifying what your brain is deeming as a threat in the first place!

Label the feeling, label the threat, challenge the negative thought!

What do athletes see as a threat?

So, you now have an understanding of anxiety and fear and how they are your response to a perceived threat. What does this mean in terms of your performance?

Well, have you ever felt distracted before a game, worrying about what could go wrong, feeling jittery, noticing your heart racing, and finding yourself thinking about the worst case scenario? "Uh oh! What if I make a mistake today?"

Most athletes have felt this way before. Often, the more importance we put on a performance, the more we feel this worry. Remember, these symptoms are your body working correctly. The first step is to remind yourself that you are okay. Take a deep breath and explore what your brain is perceiving as a threat.

What are these threats?

• *Playing time*	• *Not being 'good enough'*
• *Making the starting lineup*	• *Self-worth*
• *Opinion of others*	• *Competition*
• *Making mistakes*	• *Injury*
• *Losing*	

These perceived threats create the anxiety response in our body, and we begin to fear these as real outcomes. Our thoughts zero in on these threats becoming true until we convince ourselves they are inevitable and we need to then fear our performance.

Remember earlier in this section, when we shared that our brains are terrible at predicting the future? This is true in our performance outcomes as well. Our brain has no real idea how this performance will go. If we fail to give it a path to follow, it will most likely go to "uh oh" thinking.

Knowing our brain will respond to a threat with anxiety, we can now start to do the work for ourselves to create different thoughts around performance. We can do this through our self-talk and through our visualization prior to stepping on the field, or court, before jumping in that pool and before stepping on to the track. We will explore both of these areas later in the workbook.

MY ANXIETY DIARY

We each feel anxiety in different ways. Some of us notice it in our thoughts first while others feel a physical response to begin with.

RECORD HOW ANXIETY INFLUENCES EACH AREA BELOW.

THOUGHTS	PHYSICAL

HOW DO YOU MANAGE YOUR ANXIETY:

Check which applies. Write in your own if not listed.

- ☐ Deep Breathing
- ☐ Limiting Social Media
- ☐ Exercise
- ☐ Visualization
- ☐ Talking to Someone
- ☐ Avoiding situations

- ☐ Meditation
- ☐ Self-Talk
- ☐ Yoga
- ☐ Thought Journal
- ☐ Gratitude
- ☐ _____

- ☐ _____
- ☐ _____
- ☐ _____
- ☐ _____
- ☐ I have no strategy

Faulty Thinking

Faulty Thinking, or the fancier terminology, Cognitive Distortions, refer to how we make sense of the world around us. These are based on our worldview, which influences our perception through numerous factors, including:

- Gender
- Race
- Socio-economic levels
- Education
- Family
- Television, Books, Social Media Friends
- Religion
- Politics
- and more

Whether you realize it or not, all of these factors influence how you view others, how you deal with challenges, how you see setbacks, and how you understand yourself within our world.

For example, you may be more apt to think you are in control of your success if you have been given opportunities to grow in response to your hard work. Someone else may feel differently if they work just as hard but never see the positive outcome.

Faulty thinking derives from irrational beliefs about yourself and the world around you, that over time, get reinforced by your own thoughts, until you eventually believe these beliefs to be based in reality.

This can be seen in athletics after you lose a game. Often, the messaging in your head after a loss is, "I was terrible today and that loss was my fault!", or something close to that. In reality, you and your team probably had some ups and some downs in the contest. Yet, your brain focuses only on the negatives. This Faulty Thinking pattern is called Filtering, where we forget about any positive moments and only recall the negative.

On the next page, we will explore the most common Faulty Thinking Patterns and you can self-assess which ones you notice most in your life.

FAULTY THINKING RATING

RATING SCALE

Label each thought pattern with a 1, 2, or 3.
(1 = rarely, 2 = sometimes, and 3 = often)

FILTERING | Focusing only on the negative and forgetting the positive

OVERGENERALIZATION | Assuming all people/ experiences are the same based on one negative occurrence

CATASTROPHIZING | Assuming the worst case scenario is true; maximizing the negative

CONTROL FALLACIES | Believing everything that happens to you is all your fault or not your fault at all

BLAMING | Pointing at others for the cause of any negative events in your life

EMOTIONAL REASONING | *"I believe it, so it must be true"*

ALWAYS BEING RIGHT | Believing it is unacceptable to be wrong

POLARIZED THINKING | Not seeing the gray area in situations, it is either one or the other completely

JUMPING TO CONCLUSIONS | Thinking something is true before gathering facts or supporting evidence

PERSONALIZATION | Believing the negative occurrences around you are your fault

FALLACY OF FAIRNESS | Being too concerned over whether everything is fair

SHOULDS | Having personal rules of how people should behave and how you should be

FALLACY OF CHANGE | Expecting others to change to meet your needs or desires

What patterns did you notice most in your thinking?

There are a few take aways from this exercise that can be useful. One of the most empowering reminders before we break it down further is the following concept:

What we are aware of, we are able to manage, but what we are unaware of, manages us!

This idea celebrates the importance of self-awareness, even when it comes to faulty thinking. Once you know what you are doing, you are better able to label it as productive or unproductive for your goals.

Secondly, your thoughts and emotions are tough to understand. You know they exist, but since they are not tangible, meaning you cannot hold on to them, it is difficult to make sense of how they affect you. So, being able to put a name to these Faulty Thinking Patterns allows you to label them as they occur. Instead of believing the worst possible outcome is going to happen, you can instead remind yourself, "I am just catastrophizing."

Being able to name the pattern, allows you space to analyze your thought process and choose to see the situation in a different way.

Finally, this exercise is powerful because it reminds you these patterns are not just affecting you. They have names and descriptions because they are present in all of us. I teach these on a daily basis, but it does not make me immune to them.

So, what do you do with this knowledge?

There are some quick hitting strategies in the moment to help you work through the obstacles these thought patterns create. Two questions I love to introduce to my clients are:

1. Is this thought based on fact or opinion?
2. What advice would I give to a friend in this situation?

Both of these questions allow your rational brain to come back to working order and they again provide you space to operate on a mental level. Most of us give really good advice to others, so asking this question usually paves a path for you to follow. Also, admitting your thought is only based in opinion allows you to then explore other possible opinions as well. If worst-case is possible, so is best-case!

The next page is a Faulty Thinking Tracker worksheet to explore this further. List the faulty thinking type you had, when you had it and create a replacement thought that challenges the negative thought your brain is telling you.

FAULTY THINKING WORKSHEET

FOR THE WEEK OF | _____
MONTH/DAY

SITUATION : _____

FAULTY THINKING TYPE : _____

REPLACEMENT THOUGHT:

SITUATION : _____

FAULTY THINKING TYPE : _____

REPLACEMENT THOUGHT:

SITUATION : _____

FAULTY THINKING TYPE : _____

REPLACEMENT THOUGHT:

REMINDERS

1. You are most efficient when your mental, emotional and physical energy are used effectively. Faulty thinking spends valuable mental and emotional energy!
2. Our thoughts guide our behaviors. If you want to change your behaviors, restructure your thoughts to be purposeful, productive and positive.
3. This is a skill that takes practice to strengthen. Do not be too hard on yourself! This exercise is merely to bring awareness to thought processes we already utilize and to determine if they are helping or hindering our success.

Process vs Result

I was in a college soccer team locker room for a pre-season game. I had been working with the coach of the team for two weeks at this point and he invited me to join them for their pre-game talk. He was positive, energetic, team-oriented, and engaging. The team was attentive and driven. The main focus of his talk was the team goal for the day, a shutout. We need to get a shutout today, we will get a shutout today, a shutout is our goal!

In my work with other coaches, teams and athletes, I hear goals like the ones above often.

These are what we refer to as Result Oriented goals. They focus on an outcome, and most often these create higher levels of anxiety and stress. In addition, if we focus only on Result Oriented goals, we are connecting your sense of self to an outcome. You are deciding if you are good enough solely on the final product.

In adopting an optimistic, resilient, and gritty mindset, you are committing to the joy of the journey. You embrace the fact that you are on a continual path of improvement, competing against yourself each day. Comparing ourselves to others only gives us false hope, or self-doubt.

Being Process-Oriented means you understand each day teaches you and helps you grow towards your ultimate goal. This also means falling in love with the success and the failures along the way; realizing each one plays an important role in your future achievement.

This reminds me of a line from the poem, "IF" by Rudyard Kipling:

If you can meet with Triumph and Disaster

And treat those two impostors just the same;

These two lines are ones I repeat to myself often. You see, results are fleeting (good results and bad results, successes and failures), meaning the second they happen, they are gone. Therefore, focusing solely on results can actually stop you from moving forward.

Success can be just as hindering as failure. For example, when we win, we forget to ask ourselves what led to that win. We simply enjoy the feeling of winning and walk away thinking we are good enough. Conversely, when we lose, we forget to ask ourselves what led to that result and what we can change for next time. We simply walk away feeling like we are not good enough.

Process vs Result

Success and failure can both be equal teachers in our journey of becoming if we are willing to listen to their lessons!

When we are purely result driven, we tend to rest and think we arrived with success, and we tend to quit and think we can never make it (catastrophizing) when we fail.

Learning how to cope with setbacks now can make us stronger moving forward. Our brain will be less anxious about mistakes and failure because we have given it examples of how we can respond positively to the ups and downs of performance.

Many of us can identify the youth athlete who was the most athletic, the fastest, the strongest. They picked up every sport, and were always the best. But, often, this athlete eventually struggles when they get to higher levels. Why? If success is easy for them, and they have equated results to their self-value, the young successful athlete who never has to deal with adversity eventually gets tested for the first time. They go from invincible to destroyed in a matter of one game, their self-worth getting a significant challenge for the first time and having no strategy to deal with the thoughts and emotions that accompany failure.

The truth, however, lies in the balance. A success, in the moment, provides us feedback on how to keep moving forward. Ask the question, how can I replicate this more consistently? How can I create the situation again?

A failure, or setback, teaches us that either the pathway was wrong or we did not employ the correct skill, or maybe, we employed the right skill at the wrong time. Either way, the setback still gives us information and feedback. If we are willing to ask ourselves, "now what?" we will be able to move past any setback.

So, back to the examples at the beginning of this lesson. Why are result oriented goals dangerous to our development, and to our success?

Go back to the coach's goal for a shutout. In this example, I counted how many times the coach mentioned shutout. He reaffirmed this goal 6 times in the 20-minute pregame talk.

A shutout was the expectation and it was how the players were to measure if they were successful or not.

In this game, the team I was observing gave up a goal 10 minutes into the game. The players, from the keeper to the forwards, were destroyed. You could see it in their body language, and the frustrations were heard in their voices, blame came quickly around the field. They struggled to regain composure and ended up conceding another goal in the next 7 minutes.

Now, down 0-2, the team was desperate for halftime to stop the bleeding.

The result goal hindered the player response to a setback. In this example, the failure to get a shutout was compounded by them also not scoring a goal in the first 15 minutes as well.

I am as competitive as they come. I don't even let my four-year old twins win in a game of Candy Land. The shift from process-oriented thinking from result-oriented thinking is to allow you to become a stronger performer. I am not telling you to be less competitive.

In fact, focusing on the process will allow you to be more competitive over a longer period of time, on a more consistent basis. Setbacks in the moment will be met with solution-focused thought instead of panic.

Result-oriented thinking forces you to only see the short-term, creating more anxiety and fear. When you feel like your result is threatened, the fear causes you to lash out in anger, to run from the challenge, to focus on the problem instead of the solution.

So, embrace a process-oriented mentality. Know you are on your journey to discover your best self! This journey has no time limit and does not need to be rushed. The successes, the failures, the joys, and the disappointments all serve a valuable role in leading you to your own personal greatness!

Snags

In the journey to perform at your highest level, you will undoubtedly come across setbacks. Sometimes these setbacks are the circumstance you find yourself in. Sometimes however, the setbacks reside within your emotional, mental, or physical approach as well. At MBS Performance Counseling, we refer to these as snags, because quite literally, you can get snagged by a negative mindset. This snag can unravel all of the other positive work you have done physically and technically.

Your internal snags can be cognitive (our thoughts), emotional, or behavioral. Sometimes our snags can be external, whether it be an individual, group, or circumstance. Even with an external snag, you have the power of choosing how you interpret it, how you process it, and how you respond to it.

When meeting with athletes one-on-one, or even with teams, we spend a good amount of time identifying your snags. We have to first know what holds you back and what distracts you from your peak performance, before we can develop strategies on how to overcome them. So, take a second to think about what distracts you from being your best.

How do you overcome your snags? We utilize the model below to help you detach from your snags. An important reminder, detachment is not quitting or giving up. It is a purposeful, active process of letting go of what you cannot control. It is staying calm in the midst of setbacks, adopting a "it is what it is" mentality for what is out of your control. Finally, it is refocusing your mind on what IS in your control, which is usually how you choose to respond to the snag.

Detachment from Snags

Separate the thinker from the thought and the feeler from the feeling

Activating Event → Action Thought Emotion → Consequence

What part is not under your control?
What part is under your control?
Utilize self-talk or a mantra after an activating event

In analyzing your detachment, it is important to first identify the activating event. What is the actual trigger for your negative response? For example, one athlete I work with has difficulty dealing with mistakes by his teammates. Another athlete identified poor decisions by the referee as a snag, while another said his own mindset when he is not in the starting lineup was a major snag of his.

The next step is to explore your current feeling, thoughts, and behaviors that occur after the activating event. What do you think, what do you feel, and what do you do? Finally, what is the consequence of your feelings, thoughts, and actions? How do these affect your performance? Is it a negative or positive affect on your performance?

Remember, consequence can be positive or negative.

Where do you have control in this sequence? Many people answer the middle column (thoughts, feelings, actions) yet, you are not in control of those if you do not control the moment directly after the activating event.

Think about the first arrow. Yes, it signifies the order of events, but it also can be looked at as the space between. This space is the time between the Activating Event and your response to it. In order to manage the space between, you must first prepare before you are faced with the activating event. You choose how you want to respond to a circumstance, or how you want to respond to your own thoughts. This is why it is so important to define, and visualize, your positive response. What is your self-talk prior to and immediately after the activating event? Own the space between! The more space you give yourself to take in the moment and choose how to respond, the more often you will respond in a solution-focused and positive manner. The more you can step back and separate yourself from the moment the clearer you can analyze this process. We call this separating the thinker from the thought and the feeler from the feeling. When you are caught in the middle of your own viewpoint, you may not see the whole picture and it is sometimes difficult to find a solution. When you step back however, and train yourself to see the situation from an outside viewpoint, you get a clearer picture of effective and appropriate reactions, allowing you to remain solution-focused and balanced in your decision making. On the next page, you can track your own Snags and work through an alternate, more productive response.

IDENTIFY YOUR SNAGS

WEEK OF | _____

PREPARED?	ACTIVATING EVENT

THOUGHTS, EMOTIONS, ACTIONS

OUTCOME

PREPARED?	ACTIVATING EVENT

THOUGHTS, EMOTIONS, ACTIONS

OUTCOME

IMPORTANT REMINDERS

- Activating events are usually out of your control.
- By recognizing the emotions, thoughts and actions that occur after an activating event, you can better plan how you want to react
- Own the space between the Activating Event in order to control Your Reaction.
- Prepare for how you want to respond. As you track your snags, be honest with yourself if you were properly prepared prior to the event.

Daily Performance Plan: Pillar 4

"Hard work outweighs talent every time. Mamba mentality is about 4 a.m. workouts, doing more than the next guy and then trusting in the work you've put in when it's time to perform. Without studying, preparation and practice, you're leaving the outcome to fate. I don't do fate." – Kobe Bryant

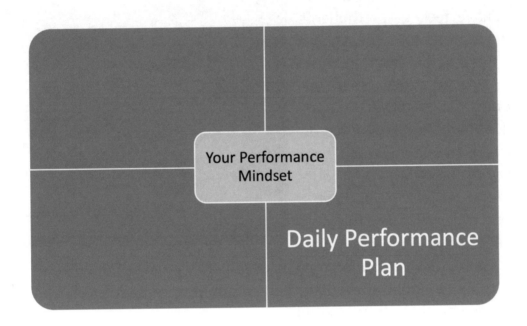

Self-Talk

You can use self-talk during a game/practice as in the example above, as well as pre-competition and post-competition in reflection.

In pre-competition, you want to instill a sense of excitement, preparedness, belief, and purpose in your self-talk. You want to remind yourself you are ready for this moment and your training has prepared you for the task at hand.

I also believe your self-talk can acknowledge any negative feelings or thoughts you are having in order to address them and reframe them before the match begins. Another way to explain this concept, is ignoring the negative thoughts does not solve them. Pretending we do not think, or feel, a certain way is a very temporary way of dealing with unproductive thoughts and feelings. If you have a younger sibling, you understand this well. What happens when you ignore a younger brother or sister? They get louder, they poke you, they jump up and down in front of you. They will get your attention! Our thoughts and emotions operate the same way. If we ignore them, they will eventually get our attention.

Your self-talk can acknowledge that you are feeling doubt, that you are afraid, that you are nervous. The key is how you respond to this acknowledgment. This is where you can ask yourself, "What would I say to a friend?"

This important question allows you to step outside your own perception and rationalize the advice you would give to another person. If you are like most people, you give amazing advice to others that you do not always follow yourself.

If a friend says, "I am worried I will not perform well in tomorrow's game", what would you say to them? Maybe something along the lines of, "You will be fine! You have been playing well at practice, you will be great, and I believe in you!" Now, imagine if you spoke to yourself this same way!

I was speaking to one professional athlete in a session and he said, "Before the game, I could either talk to myself about 20 mistakes or 20 successes. The 20 successes will make me more confident and lead to a better performance. So I choose to repeat this language to myself."

Along these lines, I challenge you to develop a mantra to repeat to yourself before the game and during the game (examples from athletes I have worked with, "respond", "breathe", "have fun", "I am ready", "be me", "attack", "shine"...)

Reminders for your self-talk: Be specific, repeat it often, believe in yourself, in your ability, and in your value!

As mentioned, you can also use self-talk strategies in your post-game as a reflection technique. I encourage athletes to do this quick exercise on the bus/car ride home or once you have time to calm the physical, mental, and emotional levels from competition, but soon enough while the details of the game/practice can still be recalled accurately.

> ### *The components of post-game reflection are:*
>
> - What went well? What skills, tactics, mindsets did I employ successfully?
> - How can I put myself in positions to utilize my strengths and build on what went well?
> - What are 1-2 specific decisions/skills I want to improve for next game?
> - What can I do in training, or on my own, to build on these?

Remember, be honest with yourself, but speak in kind and compassionate words for self-talk. One performance, or even multiple performances do not define what you can achieve. Each performance is another checkpoint in your process of development.

Learn from the successes and the failures!

WHAT ARE MY
WORDS SAYING?

Track your thoughts and self-talk for the day. Record them in your notebook. **Things to consider are:**

What words are you using?

What words are you not using?

Do your words create optimal emotional levels for performance?

What words do you repeat? How often?

Do your words excite or deflate you?

MBS Performance Counseling, LLC

 **WHAT ARE MY** WORDS SAYING?

Do your words make you feel prepared for competition or fearful of competition?

Are your words positive or negative?

NOW TRACK THE WORDS YOU USE WITH OTHERS.

Are they similar to your self-talk?

How do your words differ to others?

What are words saying when you are winning? Losing?

After a success? After a setback?

Performance Persona

The Performance Persona can be one of the more powerful performance exercises you can do. As we break it down, you will see how simple it really is and this is exactly the point.

You have enough to think about on game day and during your performance. The majority of what we are sharing with you through this workbook is to be used prior to performance to allow your mind to focus on your process goals.

The Performance Persona is one of those pre-performance tools that organizes your self-talk and visualization into tidy, digestible, and easily accessible phrases. The Performance Persona card on the next page provides a great way to organize these statements so you can print it out and take it with you in the car or bus to use on the way to games.

First, I want you to think about the words that describe you when you are at your best. Explosive, resilient, active, fast, relentless, motivated, confident, etc. List your 3 performance words on the card in the lines after "I am..."

Unpack these words by asking yourself, "If someone was to watch me play today, what would I be doing for them to label my play as ___explosive___?"

Next, you will think of an image that embodies you at your best. For an example, I had a boxer I was working with and he identified this image as a lion. Internally I thought this makes sense, strong and attacking. But, when I voiced this out-loud to him, he nodded and then stated, "There is more to it though."

He went on to explain the image of a lion reminded him that he is the king of the jungle, and the boxing ring was his jungle. His competitor was trying to enter his home, to take what was already his, and he wanted to defend his home with strength, ferocity, and poise.

Once you have your performance words and the image to go along with them, you want to create affirmation statements that remind you that these words embody your spirit. Use some of the examples on the next page:

MBS Performance Counseling, LLC

- "I am confident. I am prepared and ready for this challenge. I trust myself to make quick decisions in order to play decisively. I can do this?

- "I am explosive. I commit to my movements and make them with power and strength?

The Performance Persona allows you to organize your self-talk into specific statements, that when you repeat them, also help you visualize these very skills in your performance. Your brain can be trained to be confident, to be solution-focused and to be resilient. Committing to this exercise and repeating these words to yourself on a daily basis will train your brain to be ready to meet the demands of performance!

PERFORMANCE
PERSONA CARD

_____ 'S PERFORMANCE

PERSONA CARD

_____

I am _____ , _____ ,

and _____.

I am a _____

WHAT ARE 3 STATEMENTS THAT HELP DEFINE MY PERFORMANCE PERSONA?

1 | _____

_____

2 | _____

_____

3 | _____

_____

Visualization

Now, we will explore how Positive Visualization connects with self-talk; priming you for your optimal level of performance.

The clearer you can see your desires, the more likely you are to achieve them. The goal is to get your thoughts, emotions, and behaviors on the same frequency as the dreams you have. Your imagination is a powerful tool in that it can accomplish as much as you ask of it as long as you give it time, attention, and space to operate. Often, we stifle our own imaginations through pessimistic thoughts under the shroud of being "real".

So, build your castle in your dreams first! Use positive self-talk, imagine the process as well as the finished product, think positively and imagine solutions to problems that may arise. Be resilient in your vision, even when your own mind tries to tell you it isn't possible. And finally, enjoy the journey that your dreams take you on. No dream is too big!!

But, does visualization actually help your athletic performance?

VISUALIZATION

The answer is a resounding YES, and here is why:

First, there is research that shows your brain cannot differentiate between a real and imagined memory. Therefore, you can use visualization to prepare the brain and actually regulate how it reacts in times of stress. What this means is practicing visualization allows you to reduce anxiety by "living" the experience before it happens.

Since anxiety is the fear of the unknown, visualizing the upcoming event allows it to be known in the brain and we can recall the practiced reaction in the moment.

A swimmer may visualize herself standing on the starting block prior to a race. She can hear the fans in the crowd, the echo inside the pool, and the chatter of the other swimmers around her. She smells the chlorine from the pool and feels the familiar sensation of her swim cap and goggles on her head and face. She sees herself releasing quickly when the gun goes off, hitting the water at the perfect angle. She pauses her visualization here, seeing her hands, torso, legs and feet. She notices her position, takes note and 'presses play' to restart the visualization. She can feel her hands, then her head, and the rest of her body breaking the surface of the water. Once she begins the strokes, she can feel the movement of her arms, the power of her movements. She can feel the breaths she is taking as she flies down her lane towards the other wall. When she gets to the end of the race, she pictures herself looking up, smiling, seeing her target time.

This visualization practice allows the brain to feel comfortable with the upcoming meet. The initial thoughts around the competition might be "uh oh" or "I hope I don't lose." These thoughts only get stronger if we let them grow without challenging them. Visualization allows us to show the brain that you are okay and it gives the brain a clear picture on what to expect. The brain feels more comfortable and fears the competition less when the event is no longer this scary, unknown entity in our mind.

VISUALIZATION STRATEGIES

LEARNING ATHLETIC TECHNIQUE

IMITATE | Watch the skill performed by others who have mastered it.

MINIMIZE | Break the skill down into individual steps.

ANTICIPATE | Visualize the scenario where the technique would be used.

GRADUAL SKILL VISUALIZATION | Visualize completing each step successfully.

ENTIRE SKILL VISUALIZATION | Visualize completing skill in scenario successfully.

SET THE STAGE!

1 | Be specific! Visualize the exact field you will be playing on. Who is there? What do you hear? What do you smell? What do feel, physically and emotionally?

2 | Do your thoughts and emotions line up with your vision? If not, do the work and make them get in sync. What needs to change? Be specific and take action!

3 | What will success feel like? How will you think and feel once the game is over and success is yours?

PERFORMANCE IN MATCHES

PREPARATION | Visualize arriving to the game, putting on your uniform, etc.

PRE-GAME | Develop pregame mental routine; create positive emotions.

POST-GAME | Reflect. What went well? What are 1-2 areas for growth?

POSITIVE PLAY | Visualize succeeding in the game, specific skills, outcomes.

Visualization

As you can see, visualization can go very in depth! Have fun with it! The more detail you can incorporate into your visual practice, the more real it is for your brain. Which means, the more it associates the visual to life!

When we visualize a skill or an action, the same area of the brain is stimulated that would be if you were actually performing the skill. A study with golfers showed an hour of visualization practice was just as effective as 30 minutes of actual practice. Doing both, physical practice and visualization, is more effective than doing either one alone. Visualization increases optimism and resilience while also enhancing motivation, increasing confidence and improving motor function of an athlete. Looking ahead, we will discuss the Flow Model in a future lesson and visualization is a powerful practice for increasing your ability to enter a state of flow or your optimal zone of performance.

As you embrace the power of visualization, here are a few tips for you to get started:

- Develop a purposeful practice of visualization for daily use.
- Know what you want to accomplish and visualize how to do it.
- Describe your vision.
    o   Utilize all of your senses (sight, smell, touch, hearing).
    o   Explore your emotions and how to spark the ideal ones.
- See your performance through your own eyes – personalizing the visualization.
- Break down skills into step-by-step visuals. Then, build it back up so you can visualize the parts of the skill as well as the whole skill.
- These same skills work for preparing your athletic self, as well as your academic self and social self.

I love this quote from the Brazilian soccer player Ronaldinho:

"When I train, one of the things I concentrate on is creating a mental picture of how to best deliver the ball to a teammate, preferably leaving him alone in front of the rival goalkeeper. So what I do, always before a game, always, every night and every day, is try and think up things, imagine plays, which no one else will have thought of, and to do so always bearing in mind the particular strength of each team-mate to whom I am passing the ball. When I construct those plays in my mind I take into account whether one team-mate likes to receive the ball at his feet, or ahead of him; if he is good with his head, and how he prefers to head the ball; if he is stronger on his right or his left foot. That is my job. That is what I do. I imagine the game."

MBS Performance Counseling, LLC

Emotional Compass

The Emotional Compass has become one of my favorite exercises to work through with athletes!

You spend hours, days, weeks, months and years on your physical craft as an athlete. You practice skills, running/conditioning, lift weights, speed, agility, and tactical understanding.

But how often do you pay attention to your emotional preparation and how this can benefit your performance? Do you know which emotions are present when you play your best? Do you which ones hinder your performance?

You can usually express these pretty quickly when we start to have the discussion. However, where the work comes into a practical strategy is the understanding of how to create these emotions on purpose!

Look at the worksheet on the next page. The Emotional Compass diagram is broken up into four quadrants. The top half represents High Arousal emotions (excitement, confidence, anxiety, anger, etc), while the bottom half represents Low Arousal emotions (peaceful, calm, burnout, lethargic, etc). Depending on your sport, you may want to create a specific arousal level to perform your best.

For example, a golfer may want to create more low arousal emotions for their performance while a linebacker in football may want to have more high arousal emotions in their performance.

Now imagine waking up on game day, if there was a needle pointing at one of the quadrants, or one of the specific emotions on the circle, where is that needle pointing?

Maybe it is pointing to the red zone, specifically anxiety.

But, in our conversation, you identified the orange zone, specifically confident as your ideal performance emotion. So, your needle is pointing at anxiety, but we need to move it to confident. What strategies help you do this?

This is where we tie in the lessons from previous sections. Can we utilize purposeful self-talk, visualization, and the performance persona to move that needle? Does music, a quote, an image, or watching highlight videos help move your needle?

Reflect on these questions and develop your own practice of identifying where you are on the emotional compass for practice and games (can work for taking tests in school too) and then develop your plan for how to move that needle to your desired zone!

Do you perform your best when at high or low energy state?

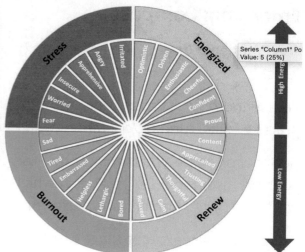

What quadrant encompasses the emotions that are best for your performance?

If we thought of the above image as a compass, with a needle pointing at how we are feeling right now, where would your needle be pointing?

How do you move your needle to your ideal zone (Self-talk, visualization, music, physical activity?

Reflection: Do you consistently check into your emotional state prior to your performance? If not, add a check in to identify your emotional zone along with a few activities to move your needle closer to your ideal zone!!

MBS Performance Counseling, LLC

Game Day Mindset

All of the work we have put in thus far has been building to this match day mindset. You took a deeper look into yourself while developing your Why and understanding your worldview. You learned the value of an optimistic mindset and to apply this way of thinking in your life on and off the field. We discussed the need to be resilient, gritty, and mentally tough. You took a glimpse into your own leadership style, and had an honest look at your snags.

As mentioned, each of these components lead to your ability to prepare yourself for competition, whether it be training or a match. How can you make sure that your emotional and mental state are at the level that allow you to perform at your best?

Your game mentality can be split into three areas.

1. Pre-Game
2. Warm-Up
3. In-Game

For each of the above, it is important to find out what works for you. Below are multiple areas to think about. When we work with clients in individual sessions we explore what works for you specifically. I ask that you self-reflect on what will benefit you as an individual. There is no one way to prepare, but each of the strategies shared in this lesson have their benefits.

Pre game = Tap into your why, create alignment, use your performance persona, visualization, and emotional compass.

I encourage you to revisit your WHY before competition. Know what fuels you and choose to compete for the bigger picture. Choose to compete with passion, purpose and a personal spirit that only your individual WHY can fuel. This is true when you step on the field for training or a match. Turn your Why into a quick hitting mantra, or create a Performance Word for yourself that primes your mind for competition. What are your expectations, what ignites you to play and what motivates you (feel these, embrace these, and let these all come alive within you)!

Do you feel that buzz of excitement? Maybe the same buzz when you watch an inspirational movie or read an inspirational quote? Take a minute to feel that energy...where does it live within you? Do you feel it in your heart? Your chest, your stomach? Your head? Do you feel it tingling in your toes and in your hands? Close your eyes and picture this energy. What color is it? Does it have a shape? Is it contained or is it spreading?

GAME DAY MINDSET

When we can create specific emotions and energy out of our WHY, we can manage our emotional preparation for games. Your WHY serves as your foundation from which we build this next step.

Now, each person's energy may be different. For some athletes, they are at their best when they have high energy, ready to go to battle. For others, though, they are creating a quieter, calmer energy that balances them.

What is your ideal state and does your WHY help create that?

Really, your ability to perform relies on your ability to create a balance in your thoughts, emotions and behavior on a consistent basis, and especially leading up to a match.

The Performance Alignment is a concept that looks at performance as an expression of how your thoughts, feelings, and behaviors interact with each other. If these are out of alignment, then you can experience more negative anxiety and stress. You will be spending valuable mental, emotional and physical energy to deal with these during the performance, which will distract you from being your absolute best on the field. Inner harmony of these three allows for optimal performance!

Entering the zone of optimal performance requires you to understand not just your ideal mentality but also your ideal emotional state. This chart represents an Individual Zone of Optimal Functioning in soccer players. Each one of us has emotional states that allow us to function at our highest level. Some of the emotions that help us are often described as negative emotions. For example, notice how tense and dissatisfied are emotions that lead to optimal zones in these athletes, whereas a normally positive emotion such as easy going and comfortable actually leads to a lesser performance.

What emotions are associated with your best performances?

So, to start trying to understand your ideal emotional state use the Performance Feedback Chart to rate your thoughts and emotions post-training or games to get an understanding of your emotional state prior to that competition, comparing it to your actual level of performance.

In addition, think about the positive and negative emotions associated with a positive performance, what are they? Think about the positive and negative emotions associated with a negative performance, what are these?

MBS Performance Counseling, LLC

PERFORMANCE FEEDBACK   WEEK OF | _____

ATHLETIC RATING | List and rate the productive emotions for your performance.

	1	2	3	4

_____

_____

_____

_____

_____

_____

_____

WHAT WENT **WELL?**	WHAT WOULD YOU LIKE TO **IMPROVE?**

What intensity of these emotions is ideal for you in setting your Individualized Zone of Performance? Do you need to be calmer (low arousal) or intense (high arousal) or somewhere in between to be at your best? Once you identify arousal levels and emotions that help your performance, it's time to figure out strategies to create these emotions.

So, once you understand your optimal emotional state for competition, there are some other strategies to employ as well as you create your pregame mentality.

1. Be singularly focused.
2. Narrow your focus – Knowing what to focus on and when to do so.
3. Embrace positive self-talk.
4. Visualize! See your success.
5. Utilize music, books, video, movies, quotes that create the ideal emotional state. What has worked for you?

Warm-Up

In this time, you are focusing on the alignment piece. You have prepared your mental and emotional self. Now, you are matching the physical preparation to your mental and emotional self. You are reaffirming your performance words:

"I am resilient."

"I am strong."

"I am a wall."

"Nothing can knock me down because I am a wall, I am strong, and I am resilient."

You are getting away from your analyzation mindset and tapping into your intuition and performance mindset. This is an important transition that allows you to trust your preparation and let go, delving fully into the moment so you are narrowing your focus to the training or match only.

Routines are important here! Physical, mental, and emotional routines should be utilized so your mind knows exactly what to expect. If this changes each game, then you are spending energy adapting, instead of on the task at hand.

In-Game

Once the game begins, you have less time that you can purposefully dedicate to your mental state, since you will be dealing with the task at hand. Here are some quick hitting reminders though:

1. Enjoy the competition
2. Stay balanced
3. Remain focused
4. Let setbacks roll off you
5. Utilize positive self-talk constantly and consistently
6. Stay solution-focused
7. Play with instinct, trust your intuition, trust your gut

As mentioned, pre-game, warmup, and in game mental and emotional skills are utilized to help you enter your flow state or zone more purposefully.

But what is Flow in terms of performance? You have definitely seen it in pro athletes when it seems everything is going perfectly. They almost seem like they are putting forth little effort, but success is all but guaranteed! You may have felt this before as well. The goal is to set the stage pre-game for a higher chance and more consistent chance of entering the zone in your play.

Flow in performance is:

1. Feeling of being in complete control
2. Participation is the reward
3. Not concerned by self-evaluation
4. Goals and feedback are clear
5. Awareness and Action merge

As a competitive athlete, are you willing to push your range in training? Are you willing to push outside your comfort zone in games in order to perform at your best? Even if it is uncomfortable?

Pushing out of your comfort zone can be scary, but as mentioned, breaking the hold fear has on your decisions allows you to pursue your absolute best!

Get comfortable with the uncomfortable! Push outside your comfort zone and embrace the challenge. This will help you achieve Flow and The Zone more consistently and help you manage anxiety as well!

Remember, stress is not the enemy. How we perceive stress, manage stress and utilize stress can be the difference between reaching a flow state in competition or not.

Finally, we discussed the alignment of your personal feelings, thoughts, and actions, but there is also a team performance alignment that must occur within successful teams.

The contagion of right practice is contagious. Meaning, if you create a positive training environment for yourself where you focus on proper skill development, dedication to your craft and living by team values, your teammates are more likely to as well. If you choose to complain and cut corners, your teammates are more likely to as well.

Now, take the next steps to finalize this concept. Develop your pre-game routine, refine your personal mantra for before and during games, and define what you want to visualize in order to reach your ideal mental and emotional state.

STRATEGY MAP

IF THIS HAPPENS...	I CAN RESPOND BY...

Reflections

Congratulations on working through the introductory mindset lessons! The previous pages will help you get started in your own journey of training your mental and emotional skills. Committing to these trainings will help you perform at your highest levels more consistently. Understand, that merely reading this workbook and completing the worksheets once will not necessarily bring the change you hope to see. Just like a physical skill, you need to be consistent in training your mental and emotional skills if you want them to be powerful in your life and performance!

Our goal is to create alignment within your physical, mental and emotional energy. You know what your physical aim is, but if your mental energy is focused on negative thoughts and your emotional energy is focused on fear and anxiety, then your performance will suffer because your focus is distracted. By bringing your mental and emotional focus into alignment with your physical goals, you will be able focus all of your energy into one purpose!

You are exactly who you need to be and you can achieve whatever you can visualize in your mind. Allow yourself to challenge the fear, anxiety and doubt that stand in your way. Understand success and failure are both teachers and part of your personal journey, and give yourself space to analyze your thoughts and emotions without judgement!

The next section of this workbook contains guided pages for you to set your intentions while developing monthly, weekly, and daily goals, thoughts, and reflections. Write honestly, hold yourself accountable and enjoy the confidence and freedom that structuring your time with a purpose provides!

Daily Reflections

In the following pages you will have a chance to take a sincere look at your day-to-day habits; analyzing how you organize your time and what you hope to accomplish each day, week and month. By identifying your strengths and areas for improvement each day, you will be able to take a purposeful approach to achieving your goals!

At MBS Performance Counseling, we believe in focusing on the process of achieving our goals, instead of the end result. With that in mind we developed our planner to provide areas for self-reflection in the core components of our performance counseling philosophy. When completed fully, the planner helps you develop skills such as optimism, grit, and resilience. These skills help you to develop a growth mindset, which allows you to focus on solutions, more than problems. These are the qualities found in the top performers in athletics, education, business, science, arts, and more.

Each week is broken down into two pages. The first page focuses on your personal development, while the second page focuses you on your athletic performance. As you plan and reflect on your priorities, time management, and goals, it is important to remain honest and objective. Step outside of your thoughts and feelings, and analyze yourself from an external viewpoint. Be your own coach and push yourself beyond your current expectations!

Month _____

PERFORM WITH PURPOSE
MONTHLY PLANNING

Goals For the Month

1. _____
2. _____
3. _____
4. _____
5. _____

What is a motivational quote, lyric, or visual that will inspire me this month?

How can I utilize my strengths to achieve my goals this month?

What are 1-2 ways I can step out of my comfort zone this week?

Are there any obstacles to my goals? What are they? How will I work through them?

Week _____

PERFORM WITH PURPOSE
PERSONAL REFLECTIONS

Personal Priorities for the Month

1. _____
2. _____
3. _____

Living for my Priorities
What actions were taken to live by my priorities?

1. _____
2. _____
3. _____
4. _____
5. _____

Time Inventory
What did I spend my time on this week?

Action   Hours Spent

1. _____ _____
2. _____ _____
3. _____ _____
4. _____ _____
5. _____ _____

Did my time spent match my priorities? If not, what can I change for next week?

What were my wins for the week?

I am grateful for...

What are three actions I will take this week to help achieve my monthly goals?

1. _____
2. _____
3. _____

Week _____

PERFORM WITH PURPOSE
PERFORMANCE REFLECTIONS

What is my weekly performance word? (ex. Brave, focus, resilient)	How will my actions reflect this word?

What went well this week in my sport?

1. _____
2. _____
3. _____

Rate the following
Rate each 1-10 (lowest 1, most prepared 10)

                                       Rating

1. Motivation   _____
2. Self-talk   _____
3. Preparedness   _____
4. Confidence   _____
5. Energy   _____
6. Positive Visualization   _____
7. Ability to overcome setbacks   _____
8. Overall Performance Rating   _____

What emotional zone was I in for practice/game?

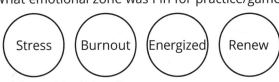

Is this my ideal Zone?

If not, what strategies will help me shift my zone to my ideal emotional state?

Positive Self-Talk, "I Will..."

What motivated me this week?

Choose a performance goal for the week. What are the process steps I can follow to achieve this goal?

Week _____

PERFORM WITH PURPOSE
PERSONAL REFLECTIONS

Personal Priorities for the Month

1. _____
2. _____
3. _____

Living for my Priorities
What actions were taken to live by my priorities?

1. _____
2. _____
3. _____
4. _____
5. _____

Time Inventory
What did I spend my time on this week?

Action	Hours Spent
1. _____	_____
2. _____	_____
3. _____	_____
4. _____	_____
5. _____	_____

Did my time spent match my priorities? If not, what can I change for next week?

What were my wins for the week?

I am grateful for...

What are three actions I will take this week to help achieve my monthly goals?

1. _____
2. _____
3. _____

Week _____

PERFORM WITH PURPOSE
PERFORMANCE REFLECTIONS

| What is my weekly performance word? (ex. Brave, focus, resilient) | How will my actions reflect this word? |

What went well this week in my sport?

1. _____
2. _____
3. _____

Rate the following
Rate each 1-10 (lowest 1, most prepared 10)

Rating

1. Motivation _____
2. Self-talk _____
3. Preparedness _____
4. Confidence _____
5. Energy _____
6. Positive Visualization _____
7. Ability to overcome setbacks _____
8. Overall Performance Rating _____

What emotional zone was I in for practice/game?

(Stress) (Burnout) (Energized) (Renew)

Is this my ideal Zone?

(Yes)   (No)

If not, what strategies will help me shift my zone to my ideal emotional state?

Positive Self-Talk, "I Will..."

What motivated me this week?

Choose a performance goal for the week. What are the process steps I can follow to achieve this goal?

Week _____

PERFORM WITH PURPOSE
PERSONAL REFLECTIONS

Personal Priorities for the Month

1. _____
2. _____
3. _____

Living for my Priorities
What actions were taken to live by my priorities?

1. _____
2. _____
3. _____
4. _____
5. _____

Time Inventory
What did I spend my time on this week?

Action	Hours Spent
1. _____	_____
2. _____	_____
3. _____	_____
4. _____	_____
5. _____	_____

Did my time spent match my priorities? If not, what can I change for next week?

What were my wins for the week?

I am grateful for...

What are three actions I will take this week to help achieve my monthly goals?

1. _____
2. _____
3. _____

Week _____

PERFORM WITH PURPOSE
PERFORMANCE REFLECTIONS

What is my weekly performance word?
(ex. Brave, focus, resilient)

How will my actions reflect this word?

What went well this week in my sport?

1. _____
2. _____
3. _____

Rate the following
Rate each 1-10 (lowest 1, most prepared 10)

Rating

1. Motivation _____
2. Self-talk _____
3. Preparedness _____
4. Confidence _____
5. Energy _____
6. Positive Visualization _____
7. Ability to overcome setbacks _____
8. Overall Performance Rating _____

What emotional zone was I in for practice/game?

Stress   Burnout   Energized   Renew

Is this my ideal Zone?

Yes   No

If not, what strategies will help me shift my zone to my ideal emotional state?

Positive Self-Talk, "I Will…"

What motivated me this week?

Choose a performance goal for the week. What are the process steps I can follow to achieve this goal?

Week _____

PERFORM WITH PURPOSE
PERSONAL REFLECTIONS

Personal Priorities for the Month

1. _____
2. _____
3. _____

Living for my Priorities
What actions were taken to live by my priorities?

1. _____
2. _____
3. _____
4. _____
5. _____

Time Inventory
What did I spend my time on this week?

Action	Hours Spent
1. _____	_____
2. _____	_____
3. _____	_____
4. _____	_____
5. _____	_____

Did my time spent match my priorities? If not, what can I change for next week?

What were my wins for the week?

I am grateful for...

What are three actions I will take this week to help achieve my monthly goals?

1. _____
2. _____
3. _____

Week _____

PERFORM WITH PURPOSE
PERFORMANCE REFLECTIONS

| What is my weekly performance word? (ex. Brave, focus, resilient) | How will my actions reflect this word? |

What went well this week in my sport?

1. _____
2. _____
3. _____

Rate the following
Rate each 1-10 (lowest 1, most prepared 10)

Rating

1. Motivation   _____
2. Self-talk   _____
3. Preparedness   _____
4. Confidence   _____
5. Energy   _____
6. Positive Visualization _____
7. Ability to overcome setbacks _____
8. Overall Performance Rating   _____

What emotional zone was I in for practice/game?

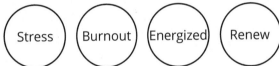

Stress   Burnout   Energized   Renew

Is this my ideal Zone?

Yes   No

If not, what strategies will help me shift my zone to my ideal emotional state?

Positive Self-Talk, "I Will…"

What motivated me this week?

Choose a performance goal for the week. What are the process steps I can follow to achieve this goal?

Month _____

PERFORM WITH PURPOSE
MONTHLY PLANNING

Goals For the Month

1. _____
2. _____
3. _____
4. _____
5. _____

What is a motivational quote, lyric, or visual that will inspire me this month?

How can I utilize my strengths to achieve my goals this month?

What are 1-2 ways I can step out of my comfort zone this week?

Are there any obstacles to my goals? What are they? How will I work through them?

MBS Performance Counseling, LLC

Week _____

PERFORM WITH PURPOSE
PERSONAL REFLECTIONS

Personal Priorities for the Month

1. _____
2. _____
3. _____

Living for my Priorities
What actions were taken to live by my priorities?

1. _____
2. _____
3. _____
4. _____
5. _____

Time Inventory
What did I spend my time on this week?

Action	Hours Spent
1. _____	_____
2. _____	_____
3. _____	_____
4. _____	_____
5. _____	_____

Did my time spent match my priorities? If not, what can I change for next week?

What were my wins for the week?

I am grateful for...

What are three actions I will take this week to help achieve my monthly goals?

1. _____
2. _____
3. _____

Week _____

PERFORM WITH PURPOSE
PERFORMANCE REFLECTIONS

| What is my weekly performance word? (ex. Brave, focus, resilient) | How will my actions reflect this word? |

What went well this week in my sport?

1. _____
2. _____
3. _____

Rate the following
Rate each 1-10 (lowest 1, most prepared 10)

                                    Rating
1. Motivation   _____
2. Self-talk   _____
3. Preparedness   _____
4. Confidence   _____
5. Energy   _____
6. Positive Visualization   _____
7. Ability to overcome setbacks _____
8. Overall Performance Rating   _____

What emotional zone was I in for practice/game?

(Stress) (Burnout) (Energized) (Renew)

Is this my ideal Zone?

(Yes)   (No)

If not, what strategies will help me shift my zone to my ideal emotional state?

Positive Self-Talk, "I Will…"

What motivated me this week?

Choose a performance goal for the week. What are the process steps I can follow to achieve this goal?

MBS Performance Counseling, LLC

Week _____

PERFORM WITH PURPOSE
PERSONAL REFLECTIONS

Personal Priorities for the Month

1. _____
2. _____
3. _____

Living for my Priorities
What actions were taken to live by my priorities?

1. _____
2. _____
3. _____
4. _____
5. _____

Time Inventory
What did I spend my time on this week?

Action	Hours Spent
1. _____	_____
2. _____	_____
3. _____	_____
4. _____	_____
5. _____	_____

Did my time spent match my priorities? If not, what can I change for next week?

What were my wins for the week?

I am grateful for...

What are three actions I will take this week to help achieve my monthly goals?

1. _____
2. _____
3. _____

Week _____

PERFORM WITH PURPOSE
PERFORMANCE REFLECTIONS

What is my weekly performance word? (ex. Brave, focus, resilient)	How will my actions reflect this word?

What went well this week in my sport?

1. _____
2. _____
3. _____

Rate the following
Rate each 1-10 (lowest 1, most prepared 10)

	Rating
1. Motivation	_____
2. Self-talk	_____
3. Preparedness	_____
4. Confidence	_____
5. Energy	_____
6. Positive Visualization	_____
7. Ability to overcome setbacks	_____
8. Overall Performance Rating	_____

What emotional zone was I in for practice/game?

Stress   Burnout   Energized   Renew

Is this my ideal Zone?

Yes   No

If not, what strategies will help me shift my zone to my ideal emotional state?

Positive Self-Talk, "I Will..."	What motivated me this week?

Choose a performance goal for the week. What are the process steps I can follow to achieve this goal?

MBS Performance Counseling, LLC

Week _____

PERFORM WITH PURPOSE
PERSONAL REFLECTIONS

Personal Priorities for the Month

1. _____

2. _____

3. _____

Living for my Priorities
What actions were taken to live by my priorities?

1. _____

2. _____

3. _____

4. _____

5. _____

Time Inventory
What did I spend my time on this week?

Action	Hours Spent
1. _____	_____
2. _____	_____
3. _____	_____
4. _____	_____
5. _____	_____

Did my time spent match my priorities? If not, what can I change for next week?

What were my wins for the week?

I am grateful for...

What are three actions I will take this week to help achieve my monthly goals?

1. _____

2. _____

3. _____

Week _____

PERFORM WITH PURPOSE
PERFORMANCE REFLECTIONS

What is my weekly performance word? (ex. Brave, focus, resilient)

How will my actions reflect this word?

What went well this week in my sport?

1. _____
2. _____
3. _____

Rate the following
Rate each 1-10 (lowest 1, most prepared 10)

Rating

1. Motivation _____
2. Self-talk _____
3. Preparedness _____
4. Confidence _____
5. Energy _____
6. Positive Visualization _____
7. Ability to overcome setbacks _____
8. Overall Performance Rating _____

What emotional zone was I in for practice/game?

Stress   Burnout   Energized   Renew

Is this my ideal Zone?

Yes   No

If not, what strategies will help me shift my zone to my ideal emotional state?

Positive Self-Talk, "I Will..."

What motivated me this week?

Choose a performance goal for the week. What are the process steps I can follow to achieve this goal?

Week _____

PERFORM WITH PURPOSE
PERSONAL REFLECTIONS

Personal Priorities for the Month

1. _____
2. _____
3. _____

Living for my Priorities
What actions were taken to live by my priorities?

1. _____
2. _____
3. _____
4. _____
5. _____

Time Inventory
What did I spend my time on this week?

Action	Hours Spent
1. _____	_____
2. _____	_____
3. _____	_____
4. _____	_____
5. _____	_____

Did my time spent match my priorities? If not, what can I change for next week?

What were my wins for the week?

I am grateful for...

What are three actions I will take this week to help achieve my monthly goals?

1. _____
2. _____
3. _____

Week _____

PERFORM WITH PURPOSE
PERFORMANCE REFLECTIONS

What is my weekly performance word? (ex. Brave, focus, resilient)	How will my actions reflect this word?

What went well this week in my sport?

1. _____
2. _____
3. _____

Rate the following
Rate each 1-10 (lowest 1, most prepared 10)

                    Rating

1. Motivation _____
2. Self-talk _____
3. Preparedness _____
4. Confidence _____
5. Energy _____
6. Positive Visualization _____
7. Ability to overcome setbacks _____
8. Overall Performance Rating _____

What emotional zone was I in for practice/game?

Stress   Burnout   Energized   Renew

Is this my ideal Zone?

Yes   No

If not, what strategies will help me shift my zone to my ideal emotional state?

Positive Self-Talk, "I Will…"

What motivated me this week?

Choose a performance goal for the week. What are the process steps I can follow to achieve this goal?

Month _____

PERFORM WITH PURPOSE
MONTHLY PLANNING

Goals For the Month

1. _____
2. _____
3. _____
4. _____
5. _____

What is a motivational quote, lyric, or visual that will inspire me this month?

How can I utilize my strengths to achieve my goals this month?

What are 1-2 ways I can step out of my comfort zone this week?

Are there any obstacles to my goals? What are they? How will I work through them?

Week _____

PERFORM WITH PURPOSE
PERSONAL REFLECTIONS

Personal Priorities for the Month

1. _____
2. _____
3. _____

Living for my Priorities
What actions were taken to live by my priorities?

1. _____
2. _____
3. _____
4. _____
5. _____

Time Inventory
What did I spend my time on this week?

Action	Hours Spent
1. _____	_____
2. _____	_____
3. _____	_____
4. _____	_____
5. _____	_____

Did my time spent match my priorities? If not, what can I change for next week?

What were my wins for the week?

I am grateful for...

What are three actions I will take this week to help achieve my monthly goals?

1. _____
2. _____
3. _____

MBS Performance Counseling, LLC

Week _____

PERFORM WITH PURPOSE
PERFORMANCE REFLECTIONS

What is my weekly performance word?
(ex. Brave, focus, resilient)

How will my actions reflect this word?

What went well this week in my sport?

1. _____
2. _____
3. _____

Rate the following
Rate each 1-10 (lowest 1, most prepared 10)

Rating

1. Motivation   _____
2. Self-talk   _____
3. Preparedness   _____
4. Confidence   _____
5. Energy   _____
6. Positive Visualization _____
7. Ability to overcome setbacks _____
8. Overall Performance Rating _____

What emotional zone was I in for practice/game?

(Stress) (Burnout) (Energized) (Renew)

Is this my ideal Zone?

(Yes)   (No)

If not, what strategies will help me shift my zone to my ideal emotional state?

Positive Self-Talk, "I Will..."

What motivated me this week?

Choose a performance goal for the week. What are the process steps I can follow to achieve this goal?

Week _____

PERFORM WITH PURPOSE
PERSONAL REFLECTIONS

Personal Priorities for the Month

1. _____
2. _____
3. _____

Living for my Priorities
What actions were taken to live by my priorities?

1. _____
2. _____
3. _____
4. _____
5. _____

Time Inventory
What did I spend my time on this week?

Action   Hours Spent

1. _____   _____
2. _____   _____
3. _____   _____
4. _____   _____
5. _____   _____

Did my time spent match my priorities? If not, what can I change for next week?

What were my wins for the week?

I am grateful for...

What are three actions I will take this week to help achieve my monthly goals?

1. _____
2. _____
3. _____

MBS Performance Counseling, LLC

Week _____

PERFORM WITH PURPOSE
PERFORMANCE REFLECTIONS

What is my weekly performance word?
(ex. Brave, focus, resilient)

How will my actions reflect this word?

What went well this week in my sport?

1. _____

2. _____

3. _____

Rate the following
Rate each 1-10 (lowest 1, most prepared 10)

	Rating
1. Motivation	_____
2. Self-talk	_____
3. Preparedness	_____
4. Confidence	_____
5. Energy	_____
6. Positive Visualization	_____
7. Ability to overcome setbacks	_____
8. Overall Performance Rating	_____

What emotional zone was I in for practice/game?

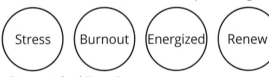

Is this my ideal Zone?

If not, what strategies will help me shift my zone to my ideal emotional state?

Positive Self-Talk, "I Will..."

What motivated me this week?

Choose a performance goal for the week. What are the process steps I can follow to achieve this goal?

Week _____

PERFORM WITH PURPOSE
PERSONAL REFLECTIONS

Personal Priorities for the Month

1. _____
2. _____
3. _____

Living for my Priorities
What actions were taken to live by my priorities?

1. _____
2. _____
3. _____
4. _____
5. _____

Time Inventory
What did I spend my time on this week?

Action	Hours Spent
1. _____	_____
2. _____	_____
3. _____	_____
4. _____	_____
5. _____	_____

Did my time spent match my priorities? If not, what can I change for next week?

What were my wins for the week?

I am grateful for...

What are three actions I will take this week to help achieve my monthly goals?

1. _____
2. _____
3. _____

Week _____

PERFORM WITH PURPOSE
PERFORMANCE REFLECTIONS

What is my weekly performance word? (ex. Brave, focus, resilient)	How will my actions reflect this word?

What went well this week in my sport?

1. _____
2. _____
3. _____

Rate the following
Rate each 1-10 (lowest 1, most prepared 10)

                            Rating

1. Motivation   _____
2. Self-talk   _____
3. Preparedness   _____
4. Confidence   _____
5. Energy   _____
6. Positive Visualization   _____
7. Ability to overcome setbacks   _____
8. Overall Performance Rating   _____

What emotional zone was I in for practice/game?

(Stress) (Burnout) (Energized) (Renew)

Is this my ideal Zone?

(Yes) (No)

If not, what strategies will help me shift my zone to my ideal emotional state?

Positive Self-Talk, "I Will…"

What motivated me this week?

Choose a performance goal for the week. What are the process steps I can follow to achieve this goal?

Week _____

PERFORM WITH PURPOSE
PERSONAL REFLECTIONS

Personal Priorities for the Month

1. _____
2. _____
3. _____

Living for my Priorities
What actions were taken to live by my priorities?

1. _____
2. _____
3. _____
4. _____
5. _____

Time Inventory
What did I spend my time on this week?

Action	Hours Spent
1. _____	_____
2. _____	_____
3. _____	_____
4. _____	_____
5. _____	_____

Did my time spent match my priorities? If not, what can I change for next week?

What were my wins for the week?

I am grateful for...

What are three actions I will take this week to help achieve my monthly goals?

1. _____
2. _____
3. _____

Week _____

PERFORM WITH PURPOSE
PERFORMANCE REFLECTIONS

What is my weekly performance word? (ex. Brave, focus, resilient)

How will my actions reflect this word?

What went well this week in my sport?

1. _____
2. _____
3. _____

Rate the following
Rate each 1-10 (lowest 1, most prepared 10)

	Rating
1. Motivation	_____
2. Self-talk	_____
3. Preparedness	_____
4. Confidence	_____
5. Energy	_____
6. Positive Visualization	_____
7. Ability to overcome setbacks	_____
8. Overall Performance Rating	_____

What emotional zone was I in for practice/game?

Stress   Burnout   Energized   Renew

Is this my ideal Zone?

Yes   No

If not, what strategies will help me shift my zone to my ideal emotional state?

Positive Self-Talk, "I Will…"

What motivated me this week?

Choose a performance goal for the week. What are the process steps I can follow to achieve this goal?

Month _____

PERFORM WITH PURPOSE
MONTHLY PLANNING

Goals For the Month

1. _____
2. _____
3. _____
4. _____
5. _____

What is a motivational quote, lyric, or visual that will inspire me this month?

How can I utilize my strengths to achieve my goals this month?

What are 1-2 ways I can step out of my comfort zone this week?

Are there any obstacles to my goals? What are they? How will I work through them?

MBS Performance Counseling, LLC

Week _____

PERFORM WITH PURPOSE
PERSONAL REFLECTIONS

Personal Priorities for the Month

1. _____
2. _____
3. _____

Living for my Priorities
What actions were taken to live by my priorities?

1. _____
2. _____
3. _____
4. _____
5. _____

Time Inventory
What did I spend my time on this week?

Action	Hours Spent
1. _____	_____
2. _____	_____
3. _____	_____
4. _____	_____
5. _____	_____

Did my time spent match my priorities? If not, what can I change for next week?

What were my wins for the week?

I am grateful for...

What are three actions I will take this week to help achieve my monthly goals?

1. _____
2. _____
3. _____

Week _____

PERFORM WITH PURPOSE
PERFORMANCE REFLECTIONS

What is my weekly performance word?
(ex. Brave, focus, resilient)

How will my actions reflect this word?

What went well this week in my sport?

1. _____
2. _____
3. _____

Rate the following
Rate each 1-10 (lowest 1, most prepared 10)

	Rating
1. Motivation	_____
2. Self-talk	_____
3. Preparedness	_____
4. Confidence	_____
5. Energy	_____
6. Positive Visualization	_____
7. Ability to overcome setbacks	_____
8. Overall Performance Rating	_____

What emotional zone was I in for practice/game?

(Stress) (Burnout) (Energized) (Renew)

Is this my ideal Zone?

(Yes)   (No)

If not, what strategies will help me shift my zone to my ideal emotional state?

Positive Self-Talk, "I Will..."

What motivated me this week?

Choose a performance goal for the week. What are the process steps I can follow to achieve this goal?

Week _____

PERFORM WITH PURPOSE
PERSONAL REFLECTIONS

Personal Priorities for the Month

1. _____
2. _____
3. _____

Living for my Priorities
What actions were taken to live by my priorities?

1. _____
2. _____
3. _____
4. _____
5. _____

Time Inventory
What did I spend my time on this week?

Action	Hours Spent
1. _____	_____
2. _____	_____
3. _____	_____
4. _____	_____
5. _____	_____

Did my time spent match my priorities? If not, what can I change for next week?

What were my wins for the week?

I am grateful for...

What are three actions I will take this week to help achieve my monthly goals?

1. _____
2. _____
3. _____

Week _____

PERFORM WITH PURPOSE
PERFORMANCE REFLECTIONS

| What is my weekly performance word? (ex. Brave, focus, resilient) | How will my actions reflect this word? |

What went well this week in my sport?

1. _____
2. _____
3. _____

Rate the following
Rate each 1-10 (lowest 1, most prepared 10)

	Rating
1. Motivation	_____
2. Self-talk	_____
3. Preparedness	_____
4. Confidence	_____
5. Energy	_____
6. Positive Visualization	_____
7. Ability to overcome setbacks	_____
8. Overall Performance Rating	_____

What emotional zone was I in for practice/game?

Stress   Burnout   Energized   Renew

Is this my ideal Zone?

Yes   No

If not, what strategies will help me shift my zone to my ideal emotional state?

Positive Self-Talk, "I Will..."

What motivated me this week?

Choose a performance goal for the week. What are the process steps I can follow to achieve this goal?

Week _____

PERFORM WITH PURPOSE
PERSONAL REFLECTIONS

Personal Priorities for the Month

1. _____

2. _____

3. _____

Living for my Priorities
What actions were taken to live by my priorities?

1. _____

2. _____

3. _____

4. _____

5. _____

Time Inventory
What did I spend my time on this week?

Action   Hours Spent

1. _____   _____

2. _____   _____

3. _____   _____

4. _____   _____

5. _____   _____

Did my time spent match my priorities? If not, what can I change for next week?

What were my wins for the week?

I am grateful for...

What are three actions I will take this week to help achieve my monthly goals?

1. _____

2. _____

3. _____

Week _____

PERFORM WITH PURPOSE
PERFORMANCE REFLECTIONS

What is my weekly performance word? (ex. Brave, focus, resilient)	How will my actions reflect this word?

What went well this week in my sport?

1. _____

2. _____

3. _____

Rate the following
Rate each 1-10 (lowest 1, most prepared 10)

Rating

1. Motivation   _____
2. Self-talk   _____
3. Preparedness   _____
4. Confidence   _____
5. Energy   _____
6. Positive Visualization _____
7. Ability to overcome setbacks _____
8. Overall Performance Rating _____

What emotional zone was I in for practice/game?

(Stress) (Burnout) (Energized) (Renew)

Is this my ideal Zone?

(Yes)   (No)

If not, what strategies will help me shift my zone to my ideal emotional state?

Positive Self-Talk, "I Will..."

What motivated me this week?

Choose a performance goal for the week. What are the process steps I can follow to achieve this goal?

Week _____

PERFORM WITH PURPOSE
PERSONAL REFLECTIONS

Personal Priorities for the Month

1. _____

2. _____

3. _____

Living for my Priorities
What actions were taken to live by my priorities?

1. _____

2. _____

3. _____

4. _____

5. _____

Time Inventory
What did I spend my time on this week?

Action	Hours Spent
1. _____	_____
2. _____	_____
3. _____	_____
4. _____	_____
5. _____	_____

Did my time spent match my priorities? If not, what can I change for next week?

What were my wins for the week?

I am grateful for...

What are three actions I will take this week to help achieve my monthly goals?

1. _____

2. _____

3. _____

Week _____

PERFORM WITH PURPOSE
PERFORMANCE REFLECTIONS

What is my weekly performance word? (ex. Brave, focus, resilient)	How will my actions reflect this word?

What went well this week in my sport?

1. _____

2. _____

3. _____

Rate the following
Rate each 1-10 (lowest 1, most prepared 10)

	Rating
1. Motivation	_____
2. Self-talk	_____
3. Preparedness	_____
4. Confidence	_____
5. Energy	_____
6. Positive Visualization	_____
7. Ability to overcome setbacks	_____
8. Overall Performance Rating	_____

What emotional zone was I in for practice/game?

Stress   Burnout   Energized   Renew

Is this my ideal Zone?

Yes   No

If not, what strategies will help me shift my zone to my ideal emotional state?

Positive Self-Talk, "I Will..."

What motivated me this week?

Choose a performance goal for the week. What are the process steps I can follow to achieve this goal?

MBS Performance Counseling, LLC

Month _____

PERFORM WITH PURPOSE
MONTHLY PLANNING

Goals For the Month

1. _____
2. _____
3. _____
4. _____
5. _____

What is a motivational quote, lyric, or visual that will inspire me this month?

How can I utilize my strengths to achieve my goals this month?

What are 1-2 ways I can step out of my comfort zone this week?

Are there any obstacles to my goals? What are they? How will I work through them?

Week _____

PERFORM WITH PURPOSE
PERSONAL REFLECTIONS

Personal Priorities for the Month

1. _____
2. _____
3. _____

Living for my Priorities
What actions were taken to live by my priorities?

1. _____
2. _____
3. _____
4. _____
5. _____

Time Inventory
What did I spend my time on this week?

Action | Hours Spent

1. _____ _____
2. _____ _____
3. _____ _____
4. _____ _____
5. _____ _____

Did my time spent match my priorities? If not, what can I change for next week?

What were my wins for the week?

I am grateful for...

What are three actions I will take this week to help achieve my monthly goals?

1. _____
2. _____
3. _____

Week _____

PERFORM WITH PURPOSE
PERFORMANCE REFLECTIONS

What is my weekly performance word? (ex. Brave, focus, resilient)	How will my actions reflect this word?

What went well this week in my sport?

1. _____

2. _____

3. _____

Rate the following
Rate each 1-10 (lowest 1, most prepared 10)

	Rating
1. Motivation	_____
2. Self-talk	_____
3. Preparedness	_____
4. Confidence	_____
5. Energy	_____
6. Positive Visualization	_____
7. Ability to overcome setbacks	_____
8. Overall Performance Rating	_____

What emotional zone was I in for practice/game?

(Stress) (Burnout) (Energized) (Renew)

Is this my ideal Zone?

(Yes)   (No)

If not, what strategies will help me shift my zone to my ideal emotional state?

Positive Self-Talk, "I Will..."

What motivated me this week?

Choose a performance goal for the week. What are the process steps I can follow to achieve this goal?

Week _____

PERFORM WITH PURPOSE
PERSONAL REFLECTIONS

Personal Priorities for the Month

1. _____
2. _____
3. _____

Living for my Priorities
What actions were taken to live by my priorities?

1. _____
2. _____
3. _____
4. _____
5. _____

Time Inventory
What did I spend my time on this week?

Action	Hours Spent
1. _____	_____
2. _____	_____
3. _____	_____
4. _____	_____
5. _____	_____

Did my time spent match my priorities? If not, what can I change for next week?

What were my wins for the week?

I am grateful for...

What are three actions I will take this week to help achieve my monthly goals?

1. _____
2. _____
3. _____

Week _____

PERFORM WITH PURPOSE
PERFORMANCE REFLECTIONS

What is my weekly performance word? (ex. Brave, focus, resilient)	How will my actions reflect this word?

What went well this week in my sport?

1. _____

2. _____

3. _____

Rate the following
Rate each 1-10 (lowest 1, most prepared 10)

Rating

1. Motivation _____
2. Self-talk _____
3. Preparedness _____
4. Confidence _____
5. Energy _____
6. Positive Visualization _____
7. Ability to overcome setbacks _____
8. Overall Performance Rating _____

What emotional zone was I in for practice/game?

(Stress) (Burnout) (Energized) (Renew)

Is this my ideal Zone?

(Yes) (No)

If not, what strategies will help me shift my zone to my ideal emotional state?

Positive Self-Talk, "I Will…"

What motivated me this week?

Choose a performance goal for the week. What are the process steps I can follow to achieve this goal?

Week _____

PERFORM WITH PURPOSE
PERSONAL REFLECTIONS

Personal Priorities for the Month

1. _____
2. _____
3. _____

Living for my Priorities
What actions were taken to live by my priorities?

1. _____
2. _____
3. _____
4. _____
5. _____

Time Inventory
What did I spend my time on this week?

	Action	Hours Spent
1.	_____	_____
2.	_____	_____
3.	_____	_____
4.	_____	_____
5.	_____	_____

Did my time spent match my priorities? If not, what can I change for next week?

What were my wins for the week?

I am grateful for...

What are three actions I will take this week to help achieve my monthly goals?

1. _____
2. _____
3. _____

Week _____

PERFORM WITH PURPOSE
PERFORMANCE REFLECTIONS

What is my weekly performance word?
(ex. Brave, focus, resilient)

How will my actions reflect this word?

What went well this week in my sport?

1. _____
2. _____
3. _____

Rate the following
Rate each 1-10 (lowest 1, most prepared 10)

                                            Rating

1. Motivation   _____
2. Self-talk   _____
3. Preparedness   _____
4. Confidence   _____
5. Energy   _____
6. Positive Visualization   _____
7. Ability to overcome setbacks   _____
8. Overall Performance Rating   _____

What emotional zone was I in for practice/game?

Stress   Burnout   Energized   Renew

Is this my ideal Zone?

Yes   No

If not, what strategies will help me shift my zone to my ideal emotional state?

Positive Self-Talk, "I Will…"

What motivated me this week?

Choose a performance goal for the week. What are the process steps I can follow to achieve this goal?

Week _____

PERFORM WITH PURPOSE
PERSONAL REFLECTIONS

Personal Priorities for the Month

1. _____
2. _____
3. _____

Living for my Priorities
What actions were taken to live by my priorities?

1. _____
2. _____
3. _____
4. _____
5. _____

Time Inventory
What did I spend my time on this week?

Action	Hours Spent
1. _____	_____
2. _____	_____
3. _____	_____
4. _____	_____
5. _____	_____

Did my time spent match my priorities? If not, what can I change for next week?

What were my wins for the week?

I am grateful for...

What are three actions I will take this week to help achieve my monthly goals?

1. _____
2. _____
3. _____

Week _____

PERFORM WITH PURPOSE
PERFORMANCE REFLECTIONS

| What is my weekly performance word? (ex. Brave, focus, resilient) | How will my actions reflect this word? |

What went well this week in my sport?

1. _____
2. _____
3. _____

Rate the following
Rate each 1-10 (lowest 1, most prepared 10)

Rating

1. Motivation   _____
2. Self-talk   _____
3. Preparedness   _____
4. Confidence   _____
5. Energy   _____
6. Positive Visualization _____
7. Ability to overcome setbacks _____
8. Overall Performance Rating _____

What emotional zone was I in for practice/game?

(Stress) (Burnout) (Energized) (Renew)

Is this my ideal Zone?

(Yes)   (No)

If not, what strategies will help me shift my zone to my ideal emotional state?

Positive Self-Talk, "I Will..."

What motivated me this week?

Choose a performance goal for the week. What are the process steps I can follow to achieve this goal?

Month _____

PERFORM WITH PURPOSE
MONTHLY PLANNING

Goals For the Month

1. _____
2. _____
3. _____
4. _____
5. _____

What is a motivational quote, lyric, or visual that will inspire me this month?

How can I utilize my strengths to achieve my goals this month?

What are 1-2 ways I can step out of my comfort zone this week?

Are there any obstacles to my goals? What are they? How will I work through them?

MBS Performance Counseling, LLC

Week _____

PERFORM WITH PURPOSE
PERSONAL REFLECTIONS

Personal Priorities for the Month

1. _____
2. _____
3. _____

Living for my Priorities
What actions were taken to live by my priorities?

1. _____
2. _____
3. _____
4. _____
5. _____

Time Inventory
What did I spend my time on this week?

Action	Hours Spent
1. _____	_____
2. _____	_____
3. _____	_____
4. _____	_____
5. _____	_____

Did my time spent match my priorities? If not, what can I change for next week?

What were my wins for the week?

I am grateful for...

What are three actions I will take this week to help achieve my monthly goals?

1. _____
2. _____
3. _____

Week _____

PERFORM WITH PURPOSE
PERFORMANCE REFLECTIONS

| What is my weekly performance word? (ex. Brave, focus, resilient) | How will my actions reflect this word? |

What went well this week in my sport?

1. _____
2. _____
3. _____

Rate the following
Rate each 1-10 (lowest 1, most prepared 10)

	Rating
1. Motivation	_____
2. Self-talk	_____
3. Preparedness	_____
4. Confidence	_____
5. Energy	_____
6. Positive Visualization	_____
7. Ability to overcome setbacks	_____
8. Overall Performance Rating	_____

What emotional zone was I in for practice/game?

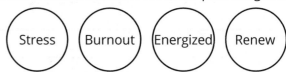

Is this my ideal Zone?

If not, what strategies will help me shift my zone to my ideal emotional state?

Positive Self-Talk, "I Will..."

What motivated me this week?

Choose a performance goal for the week. What are the process steps I can follow to achieve this goal?

Week _____

PERFORM WITH PURPOSE
PERSONAL REFLECTIONS

Personal Priorities for the Month

1. _____
2. _____
3. _____

Living for my Priorities
What actions were taken to live by my priorities?

1. _____
2. _____
3. _____
4. _____
5. _____

Time Inventory
What did I spend my time on this week?

Action	Hours Spent
1. _____	_____
2. _____	_____
3. _____	_____
4. _____	_____
5. _____	_____

Did my time spent match my priorities? If not, what can I change for next week?

What were my wins for the week?

I am grateful for...

What are three actions I will take this week to help achieve my monthly goals?

1. _____
2. _____
3. _____

Week _____

PERFORM WITH PURPOSE
PERFORMANCE REFLECTIONS

What is my weekly performance word?
(ex. Brave, focus, resilient)

How will my actions reflect this word?

What went well this week in my sport?

1. _____
2. _____
3. _____

Rate the following
Rate each 1-10 (lowest 1, most prepared 10)

	Rating
1. Motivation	_____
2. Self-talk	_____
3. Preparedness	_____
4. Confidence	_____
5. Energy	_____
6. Positive Visualization	_____
7. Ability to overcome setbacks	_____
8. Overall Performance Rating	_____

What emotional zone was I in for practice/game?

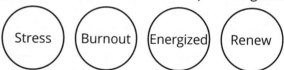

Stress Burnout Energized Renew

Is this my ideal Zone?

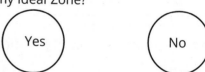

Yes   No

If not, what strategies will help me shift my zone to my ideal emotional state?

Positive Self-Talk, "I Will..."

What motivated me this week?

Choose a performance goal for the week. What are the process steps I can follow to achieve this goal?

Week _____

PERFORM WITH PURPOSE
PERSONAL REFLECTIONS

Personal Priorities for the Month
1. _____
2. _____
3. _____

Living for my Priorities
What actions were taken to live by my priorities?

1. _____
2. _____
3. _____
4. _____
5. _____

Time Inventory
What did I spend my time on this week?

Action	Hours Spent
1. _____	_____
2. _____	_____
3. _____	_____
4. _____	_____
5. _____	_____

Did my time spent match my priorities? If not, what can I change for next week?

What were my wins for the week?

I am grateful for...

What are three actions I will take this week to help achieve my monthly goals?
1. _____
2. _____
3. _____

Week _____

PERFORM WITH PURPOSE
PERFORMANCE REFLECTIONS

What is my weekly performance word? (ex. Brave, focus, resilient)	How will my actions reflect this word?

What went well this week in my sport?

1. _____

2. _____

3. _____

Rate the following
Rate each 1-10 (lowest 1, most prepared 10)

	Rating
1. Motivation	_____
2. Self-talk	_____
3. Preparedness	_____
4. Confidence	_____
5. Energy	_____
6. Positive Visualization	_____
7. Ability to overcome setbacks	_____
8. Overall Performance Rating	_____

What emotional zone was I in for practice/game?

(Stress) (Burnout) (Energized) (Renew)

Is this my ideal Zone?

(Yes)   (No)

If not, what strategies will help me shift my zone to my ideal emotional state?

Positive Self-Talk, "I Will…"	What motivated me this week?

Choose a performance goal for the week. What are the process steps I can follow to achieve this goal?

Week _____

PERFORM WITH PURPOSE
PERSONAL REFLECTIONS

Personal Priorities for the Month

1. _____
2. _____
3. _____

Living for my Priorities
What actions were taken to live by my priorities?

1. _____
2. _____
3. _____
4. _____
5. _____

Time Inventory
What did I spend my time on this week?

	Action	Hours Spent
1.	_____	_____
2.	_____	_____
3.	_____	_____
4.	_____	_____
5.	_____	_____

Did my time spent match my priorities? If not, what can I change for next week?

What were my wins for the week?

I am grateful for...

What are three actions I will take this week to help achieve my monthly goals?

1. _____
2. _____
3. _____

Week _____

PERFORM WITH PURPOSE
PERFORMANCE REFLECTIONS

What is my weekly performance word?
(ex. Brave, focus, resilient)

How will my actions reflect this word?

What went well this week in my sport?

1. _____
2. _____
3. _____

Rate the following
Rate each 1-10 (lowest 1, most prepared 10)

	Rating
1. Motivation	_____
2. Self-talk	_____
3. Preparedness	_____
4. Confidence	_____
5. Energy	_____
6. Positive Visualization	_____
7. Ability to overcome setbacks	_____
8. Overall Performance Rating	_____

What emotional zone was I in for practice/game?

(Stress) (Burnout) (Energized) (Renew)

Is this my ideal Zone?

(Yes)   (No)

If not, what strategies will help me shift my zone to my ideal emotional state?

Positive Self-Talk, "I Will..."

What motivated me this week?

Choose a performance goal for the week. What are the process steps I can follow to achieve this goal?

Made in the USA
Columbia, SC
16 November 2024

46724354R00080